The 20th Century's MOST INFLUENTIAL HISPANICS

Gabriel García Márquez

Nobel Prize–Winning Author

by Don Nardo

LUCENT BOOKS

An imprint of Thomson Gale, a part of The Thomson Corporation

THOMSON

GALE

Detroit • New York • San Francisco • San Diego • New Haven, Conn. • Waterville, Maine • London • Munich

For more information, contact:
Lucent Books
27500 Drake Rd.
Farmington Hills, MI 48331-3535
Or you can visit our Internet site at http://www.gale.com

LIBRARY OF CONGRESS CATALOGING-IN-PUBLICATION DATA

Nardo, Don, 1947-
  Gabriel García Márquez: Nobel Prize–winning author / by Don Nardo.
    p. cm. — (The twentieth century's most influential Hispanics)
  Includes bibliographical references and index.
  ISBN-13: 978-1-4205-0020-2 (hardcover)
  1. García Márquez, Gabriel, 1928—Juvenile literature. 2. Authors, Colombian—20th century—Biography—Juvenile literature. I. Title. II. Series.
  PQ8180.17.A73Z77 2007
  863'.64—dc22
  [B]
                                                                    2007024053

ISBN-10: 1-4205-0020-1

Printed in the United States of America

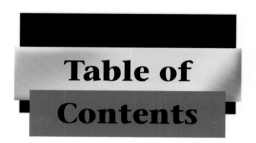

Table of Contents

Foreword

When Alberto Gonzales was a boy living in Texas, he never dreamed he would one day stand next to the president of the United States. Born to poor migrant workers, Gonzales grew up in a two-bedroom house shared by his family of ten. There was no telephone or hot water. Because his parents were too poor to send him to college, Gonzales joined the Air Force, but after two years obtained an appointment to the Air Force Academy and, from there, transferred to Rice University. College was still a time of struggle for Gonzales, who had to sell refreshments in the bleachers during football games to support himself. But he eventually went on to Harvard Law School and rose to prominence in the Texas government. And then one day, decades after rising from his humble beginnings in Texas, he found himself standing next to President George W. Bush at the White House. The president had nominated him to be the nation's first Hispanic attorney general. As he accepted the nomination, Gonzales embraced the president and said, "'Just give me a chance to prove myself'—that is a common prayer for those in my community. Mr. President, thank you for that chance."

Like Gonzales, many Hispanics in America and elsewhere have shed humble beginnings to soar to impressive and previously unreachable heights. In the twenty-first century, influential Hispanic figures can be found worldwide and in all fields of endeavor, including science, politics, education, the arts, sports, religion, and literature. Some accomplishments, like those of musician Carlos Santana or author Alisa Valdes-Rodriguez, have added a much-needed Hispanic voice to the artistic landscape. Others, such as revolutionary Che Guevara or labor leader Dolores Huerta, have spawned international social movements that have enriched the rights of all peoples.

But who exactly is Hispanic? When studying influential Hispanics, it is important to understand what the term actually means. Unlike strictly racial categories like "black" or "Asian," the term "Hispanic" joins a huge swath of people from different countries, religions, and races. The category was first used by the U.S. Census Bureau in 1980 and is used to refer to Spanish-speaking people of any race. Officially, it denotes a person whose ancestry either descends in whole or in part from the people of Spain or from the various peoples of Spanish-speaking Latin America. Often the term "Hispanic" is used synonymously with the term "Latino," but the two actually have slightly different meanings. "Latino" refers only to people from the countries of Latin America, such as Argentina, Brazil, and Venezuela, whether they speak Spanish or Portuguese. Meanwhile, Hispanic refers only to Spanish-speaking peoples but from any Spanish-speaking country, such as Spain, Puerto Rico, or Mexico.

In America, Hispanics are reaching new heights of cultural influence, buying power, and political clout. More than 35 million people identified themselves as Hispanic on the 2000 U.S. census, and there were estimated to be more than 41 million Hispanics in America as of 2006. In the twenty-first century people of Hispanic origin have officially become the nation's largest ethnic minority, outnumbering both blacks and Asians. Hispanics constitute about 13 percent of the nation's total population, and by 2050 their numbers are expected to rise to 102.6 million, at which point they would account for 24 percent of the total population. With growing numbers and expanding influence, Hispanic leaders, artists, politicians, and scientists in America and in other countries are commanding attention like never before.

These unique and fascinating stories are the subjects of The Twentieth Century's Most Influential Hispanics collection from Lucent Books. Each volume in the series critically examines the challenges, accomplishments, and legacy of influential Hispanic figures, many of whom, like Alberto Gonzales, sprang from modest beginnings to achieve groundbreaking goals. The Twentieth Century's Most Influential Hispanics offers vivid narrative, fully documented primary and secondary source quotes, a bibliography, thorough index, and mix of color and black-and-white photographs that enhance each volume and provide excellent starting points for research and discussion.

A Literary Earthquake

In the late 1920s, a boy was born into a poor family living in an obscure, poverty-stricken town near the northern coast of Colombia, a country bordering the southern Caribbean Sea. Considering the inauspicious setting of his birth, there was not the slightest hint that this shy little boy would eventually become a world-renowned author. Yet Gabriel García Márquez did in fact beat the enormous odds stacked against him. He gained fame and prestige not only for himself, but also for his country and more generally for Latin America. Success did not come easy for him, partly because he lacked money and other resources and also because he followed a winding and torturous path before finding his literary voice.

Vaulted into the Pantheon

After a long, chaotic, and difficult personal struggle, García Márquez found that special voice. And beginning in 1967, he took the international literary community by both surprise and storm. The prominent Latin American novelist Mario Vargas Llosa, who came to know him well, described the main event this way:

In about the middle of 1967, the novel *One Hundred Years of Solitude* was published in Buenos Aires [Argentina], provoking a literary earthquake throughout Latin America. The critics recognized the book as a masterpiece of the art of fiction and the public endorsed this opinion, systematically exhausting new editions, which, at one point, appeared at the astounding rate of one per week.[1]

The earthquake's tremors spread outward across the globe as *One Hundred Years of Solitude* was translated into other languages.

Gabriel García Márquez holds the Nobel Prize for Literature he was awarded in 1982.

French critics named it the best foreign book in 1969, and critics in the United States raved when the English-language version was released the following year. Throughout the 1970s, García Márquez received one honor after another, including prestigious writing awards and an honorary doctorate from Columbia University. In that same decade, he published another novel that came to be seen as a masterpiece—*The Autumn of the Patriarch*. Several of his earlier works were reprinted and translated into many languages. Then came the culmination of his career. In 1982, García Márquez was awarded the coveted Nobel Prize for Literature, vaulting him into the small but illustrious pantheon of the twentieth century's greatest writers.

Shattering Stereotypes

Acclaim by literary critics and widespread popularity among general readers are not the only reasons for García Márquez's importance in the realm of twentieth-century literature. Another reason is the enormous influence he has had on other writers, both in Latin America and elsewhere. His novels have a complex structure. There are frequent jumps forward and backward in time, for instance, and real historical events juxtaposed with fabricated ones. He also introduces numerous characters, some important, others less so, for dramatic and literary effect. "García Márquez's fiction," one literary scholar comments, "is filled with characters that come in and out of the story as a mere enunciation—as a spoken reference or part of the social scene." This approach "leads the reader to envision a whole town and its people interacting with one another as if they were all fully developed characters."[2] Many younger writers have emulated these elements of García Márquez's style in their own novels and short stories.

More than any other stylistic element, however, other writers have adopted García Márquez's use of what has come to be known as "magical realism." Put simply, it is a literary device in which fantastic occurrences, such as a person flying, are interwoven in a matter-of-fact manner into an otherwise totally realistic situation or setting. Many, if not most, other Latin American writers have explored and developed their own versions of mag-

García Márquez's literary accomplishments placed Latin American literature in the canon of great literary works.

ical realism in the years following García Márquez's huge literary success in the 1960s and 1970s.

Another of García Márquez's remarkable accomplishments has been to put Latin America in general, and Colombia in particular, on the world's literary map. Before the success of *One Hundred Years of Solitude*, Europe and the United States were widely seen as the main sources of great literature in the world. Most literary authorities considered Latin America intellectually and literarily backward, partly because the region had a reputation for being politically backward. "When I first traveled to Europe in the Fifties," García Márquez himself recalls, "I was asked, 'How can you live in such savage countries as exist in South America, where people kill one another for political reasons?'"[3]

To a remarkable degree, García Márquez managed to shatter these negative stereotypes about his native region. He brought Latin American literature to the attention of a worldwide audience as no other writer in the nineteenth or twentieth centuries had been able to do. In the words of literary critic Raymond L. Williams:

> Although Latin American writers such as Mario Vargas Llosa, Carlos Fuentes, and Julio Cortazar have been read outside the Hispanic world, none of them has a corpus [body of work] of fiction as accessible as that of García Márquez. The complex themes, structures, and techniques employed by these and many other contemporary novelists sometimes limit their readership to a relatively small group. García Márquez's accessibility has allowed him to showcase both the phenomenal quality of Latin American writing and the wonders of Latin American reality.[4]

The main instrument by which García Márquez showcased Latin American literature was his greatest masterpiece, *One Hundred Years of Solitude*. Several critics have called it the greatest novel in Spanish since Miguel de Cervantes' *Don Quixote*, published in 1615. "*One Hundred Years* is the first novel in which Latin Americans recognized themselves, that defined them, celebrated their passion, their intensity, their spirituality and superstition, [and] their grand propensity for failure," University of Pittsburgh scholar Gerald Martin remarks. "Only time will tell if he's as important to Spanish literature as Cervantes. We may have to wait 500 years to find out."[5]

Chapter 1

Ghosts of Childhood

Gabriel García Márquez came into the world on March 6 in either 1927 or 1928. No one, not even the famous writer himself, knows which year it was because at that time his tiny hometown of Aracataca, Colombia, did not issue birth certificates for newborns. More certain was that the new baby almost strangled on his umbilical cord. He was born unconscious and revived only after the midwife poured holy water on him. (Infant mortality was extremely high in Colombia in those days, and it was common practice to keep holy water on hand at births in case of an emergency. It remains uncertain whether ordinary water would have produced the same outcome.)

For a long time his parents, Luisa Santiaga Márquez Iguarán and Gabriel Eligio García, and other relatives called the child Gabito, meaning "little Gabriel," to differentiate him from his father. (Later, people all over his native land would give him an even shorter nickname, one brimming with respect and affection —Gabo.) Most people in his family had strong reasons for wanting to mark the differences between the boy and his father.

In 2007, the author arrives in Aracataca, the city where he was born.

Family Problems

The main problem was that Luisa's parents, Colonel Nicolás Márquez and Doña Tranquilina Márquez, detested their daughter's fiancé. First, Gabriel Eligio García, a young telegraph operator, was a latecomer to the town, which had been established in the late 1800s. The colonel had brought his family to Aracataca in 1911, when Luisa was five. And though they were poor, their neighbors viewed them respectfully as part of the "old blood" who had helped the town survive various crises over the years. Outsiders like García were not welcome.

Luisa's parents also disliked García because he was an itinerant, moving often from one place to another, and because he had been born out of wedlock, a badge of dishonor in a devoutly Catholic society. Another strike against Luisa's suitor was that he was known to be a womanizer who had fathered several illegitimate children. The colonel and his wife came to call García *la hojarasca*, meaning "dead leaf," suggesting that he would drift out of town on the next forceful gust of wind.

For her part, Luisa insisted that she did not care what her parents thought of her intended husband. Despite his faults, she said, she loved him because he had an artistic soul. He played the violin, enjoyed reading poetry aloud, and treated her tenderly and politely. Perhaps the García whom Luisa loved so much was captured in "a photograph from those days" that later came into his son's possession. The photo, García Márquez says,

> shows him with the equivocal air of an impoverished gentleman. He [is] wearing a suit of dark taffeta with a four-button jacket, very close-fitting in the style of

The Descendants of Pirates

In an interview he gave in 1982, García Márquez described the colorful mix of cultures in the northern section of Colombia, where his hometown of Aracataca is located.

I happen to come from the Caribbean part of Colombia, which is a fantastic place—completely different from the Andean part, the highlands. During the colonial period of Colombian history, all the people who considered themselves respectable went to the interior —to Bogotá. On the coast, all that were left were bandits— bandits in the good sense— and dancers, adventurers, [and] people full of gaiety. The coastal people were descendants of pirates and smugglers, with a mixture of black slaves. To grow up in such an environment is to have fantastic resources for poetry. Also, in the Caribbean, we are capable of believing anything, because we have the influence of all those different cultures, mixed in with Catholicism and our own local beliefs. I think that gives us an open-mindedness to look beyond apparent reality.

Quoted in Gene H. Bell-Villada, ed., *Conversations with Gabriel García Márquez*. Jackson: University Press of Mississippi, 2006, p. 112.

the day, a high stiff collar and wide tie, and a flat-brimmed straw hat. He also wore fashionable round spectacles with thin wire frames and clear lenses.[6]

However respectable García may have looked and no matter what Luisa saw in him, it was not enough to win over her father. The colonel repeatedly listed the young man's shortcomings and then added what he saw as the worst black mark of all against García. Namely, he was a conservative, whereas the colonel himself was a liberal.

A Life Shaped by Diverse Forces

The colonel's preoccupation with party affiliations was part of a huge current of cultural and political forces that lurked just beneath the surface of life in Aracataca and other Colombian towns. These diverse forces had shaped the colonel's worldview and were destined to shape the beliefs—and the world-renowned novels—of his grandson. In fact, to understand and appreciate García Márquez's writings, one must realize that his intellect, personality, and interests were molded in part by certain elements of the prevailing human condition in his native land—especially multiculturalism, violence, family and political ties, and poverty.

Among the first of these elements that García Márquez was exposed to as a small child was multiculturalism. Latin America, including Colombia, as literary scholar Ruben Pelayo points out, possesses a civilization

> where Indians, Europeans, and Africans [the descendants of black slaves brought to the Americas] have created a distinctly Latin American way of life in all its forms (literature being one of them). By the time of independence from Spain, between 1810 and 1824, most Spanish-speaking countries [in Central and South America] had integrated [many] cultures into one. This was a nationalistic experience that precipitated countless civil wars in the newly formed republics.[7]

These frequent civil wars produced another element that shaped García Márquez's character and worldview—violence, in particular neighbors fighting neighbors. Indeed, Colombia seemed to suffer from this sort of discord more than other nations in the region.

After becoming independent from Spain in 1819, at first Colombia consisted not only of the territory making up modern Colombia, but also what are now Venezuela, Ecuador, and Panama. In a series of violent spasms, Venezuela became independent from Colombia in 1821; Ecuador separated from Colombia in 1822; and in 1903, Panama did the same.

In addition to these violent episodes, Colombia suffered from almost incessant civil unrest within its own borders. The main cause was hatred and distrust between the country's two principal political parties—the conservatives and the liberals. In theory, Colombia had been established as a democracy. But the seemingly relentless feud between the two parties, which drove a wedge between Colonel Nicolás Márquez and his prospective son-in-law, spawned a series of corrupt, dictatorial regimes. "The conservatives and the liberals are more like warring factions or clans than any parties with firmly established or radically opposing ideologies," scholar Allen B. Ruch explains.

> Both tend to be repressive, both are corrupt, and both terribly abuse power when it falls into their hands; and throughout the sad history of Colombia, both parties have been more or less at war. It has often been said of Colombia's parties that you do not join them, you are born into them; and indeed they act more as territorial and familial units than as peacefully functioning parties with distinct political platforms.[8]

The Santa Marta Massacre

The two warring parties reached what many Colombians viewed as the pinnacle of their feud in 1899, not long before García Márquez's mother was born. In that year, the so-called War of a Thousand Days erupted. The conservatives were in control of the government at the time. When a serious dispute over coffee prices caused many liberal coffee farmers to go bankrupt, the country's liberals declared war on the government. During three years of savage fighting, more than one hundred thousand people lost

When Colombia gained its independence from Spain in 1819, it was part of the larger Brazilian empire, which included Venezuela, Panama, and Ecuador.

their lives. Finally, in 1902, the two sides negotiated a peace deal, but the old hatreds lingered, keeping the nation almost perpetually on the brink of further violence.

The hatreds created by the wars of the ruling parties intruded into family life in the Aracataca of García Márquez's youth. The boy's outlook on life was also profoundly affected by a more recent violent event. Between 1915 and 1918, when his mother, Luisa, was in her teens, a North American corporation—the United Fruit Company—had invested in the region. The company established banana plantations, some of them near Aracataca, which for the first and only time in its history enjoyed financial prosperity.

The banana plantations of the United Fruit Country filled the coffers of government officials in Colombia and oppressed the people who worked the plantations.

But it soon became clear that only the company's owners and a chosen few local growers were going to benefit from the good times. The workers, whose wages remained abysmally low, began protesting. In 1928, about the time that García Márquez was born, thirty-two thousand of them went on strike. The government, then controlled by the conservatives, sided with the owners because it wanted the company to keep pumping money into the country's economy. So soldiers armed with rifles appeared at a gathering of strikers in the town of Cienaga, not far from Aracataca. Tensions rose and the troops opened fire on unarmed civilians, killing thousands. García Márquez later described the slaughter, which came to be known as the Santa Marta Massacre:

> I knew the event as if I had lived it, having heard it recounted and repeated a thousand times by my grandfather from the time I had a memory. The soldier reading the decree by which the striking laborers were declared a gang of lawbreakers; the three thousand men, women, and children motionless under the savage sun after the officer gave them five minutes to evacuate the square; the order to fire, the clattering machine guns spitting in white-hot bursts, the crowd trapped by panic as it was cut down, little by little, by the methodical, insatiable scissors of the shrapnel.[9]

Memories of His Grandparents

Many of those killed in the War of a Thousand Days and the massacre at Cienaga were friends and neighbors of García Márquez's family. So it was inevitable that Colombia's and Aracataca's turbulent past would spill over into his young life and shape him in ways that he did not understand at the time. Only later, as he grew into adulthood, did he learn, a little at a time, and sometimes with pain and regret, how much a product he was of the political, financial, and social problems of the region.

García Márquez first began to learn about these problems and his connection to them through his extraordinary relationship with his grandparents. For several years they largely raised him because his parents moved away, leaving him in the care of the colonel and his wife. García Márquez later recalled that Luisa and her lover, García, were married on June 11, 1926. In a spirit of protest, Luisa's parents did not attend the ceremony. Then, in an effort to avoid friction with his in-laws, "My father took a job in another town far from Aracataca," the adult García Márquez wrote.

> When my mother became pregnant with me, in a gesture of reconciliation, my grandparents said, "Come have the baby in our house." Which she gladly did. After a while, my mother returned to the village my father was working in, and so my grandparents said, "Leave Gabriel with us to raise." The family was poor, and as I said, extended families are common in the Caribbean [region of Colombia].[10]

Showcase of Writers

"I suppose you realize the trouble you've gotten into. Now you're in the showcase of recognized writers, and there's a lot you have to do to deserve it."

——Jorge Alvaro Espinosa, quoted in Gabriel García Márquez, *Living to Tell the Tale*. Trans. Edith Grossman. New York: Knopf, 2003, p. 250.

The nearly eight years the boy spent with his grandparents became in many ways the most formative and memorable of his young life. As he wrote later, "I feel that all my writing has been about the experiences of the time I spent with my grandparents."[11] The colonel and his wife, like so many Colombian peasants of that era, were both extremely religiously devout and superstitious. They believed in a vengeful God who punished people even for minor sins, and they also believed that the ghosts of the dead haunted the living. Indeed, García Márquez later remembered, his grandparents' house was "full of ghosts." Both, he said, "were very superstitious and impressionable people. In every corner there were skeletons and memories, and after six in the evening you didn't dare leave your room. It was a world of fantastic terrors."[12]

Doña Tranquilina was a particularly devout believer in ghosts, the predictive power of dreams, and other supernatural elements. Her grandson later recalled:

García Márquez's grandmother, Doña Tranquilina, told him supernatural stories, including one of rocking chairs that moved of their own volition. These stories would later fuel García Márquez's fiction.

> She saw that the rocking chairs rocked alone, that the phantom of puerperal fever was lurking in the bedrooms of women in labor, that the scent of jasmines from the garden was like an invisible ghost. . . . She had a very personal system for interpreting her own dreams and those of others, which governed the daily behavior of each one of us and controlled the life of the house.[13]

Stories and Life's Mysteries

Both the colonel and Doña Tranquilina regularly told their young grandson stories that colored his view of the culture and the physical world he inhabited. His grandmother told tales of floating spirits and other aspects of the supernatural; his grandfather told stories of real events, filtered and colored to reflect the colonel's political beliefs. García Márquez remembers that, perhaps because he was male, he related more to his grandfather and the stories he told than to the tales told by his grandmother and the aunts who also lived in the house. The colonel "was the only person I communicated with in the house," García Márquez later wrote.

> The world of the women—it was so fantastic that it escaped me. But my grandfather brought me back to reality by telling me stories about tangible things— items from the newspapers, war stories from the time he was a colonel on the liberal side in the Colombian civil wars. Whenever my grandmother or my aunts said something particularly wild, he'd say, "Don't listen to that. Those are women's beliefs."[14]

García Márquez recalls a particularly memorable example of his grandfather's introducing him to life's tangible realities—an incident in which the old man showed him ice for the first time.

These boys wait to take a chunk of ice home for the family's icebox. García Márquez's first experience with ice found its way into one of his novels.

This proved only one of many such episodes from the writer's past that he remembers primarily because of the strong physical sensations they imparted to him. "Aracataca was a tropical town," García Márquez writes,

> and living there, as I did, in the days before refrigeration, I had never seen ice. One day my grandfather took me to the company store of the United Fruit Company . . . and he showed me a crate filled with ice-packed fish. Whatever it was that was inside the boxes was so cold that it seemed to me to be boiling. I touched the inside of the box and felt burned. "But this is boiling," I said to my grandfather. And he told me, "No, on the contrary, it is very cold." And then he gave me this substance to touch—and it was ice. [Ever since] what

A Bull in the Kitchen

Growing up in rural Colombia in the 1930s, García Márquez accumulated numerous memorable experiences that he later wrote about. One of the most dramatic was the sudden appearance of a full-grown bull in the family home.

A wild bull that had escaped the bull pens on the [town] square burst into the kitchen, bellowing like a steamship and in a blind rage charging the equipment in the bakery and the pots on the stoves. I was going in the opposite direction when the gale of terrified women lifted me into the air and took me with them into the storeroom. The bellowing of the runaway bull in the kitchen and the galloping of the hooves on the cement floor of the hallway shook the house. Without warning, he appeared in a ventilation skylight, and the fiery panting of his breath and his large reddened eyes froze my blood. When his handlers succeeded in taking him back to the bull pen, the revelry of the drama had already begun in the house and would last more than a week, with endless pots of coffee and sponge cakes to accompany the tale, repeated a thousand times.

Gabriel García Márquez, *Living to Tell the Tale*, trans. Edith Grossman. New York: Knopf, 2003, p. 36.

remain for me are flashes of memory that I hardly ana-
lyze. I prefer only the sensations they leave.[15]

The colorful childhood stories and incidents that García
Márquez associates with his grandparents were destined to stay
with him throughout his long life. They became a principal basis
of his own storytelling when he became a world-famous writer
of novels and short fiction. He came to realize that his grandparents had passed on to him certain compelling stories they had
heard when they were young; then he had found a way to pass
these tales on to his readers. About transgenerational storytelling
in his youth, he later stated: "I [constantly] wanted more. The
voracity with which I listened to stories always left me hoping for
a better one the next day, above all those [stories] that had to do
with the mysteries of [life]."[16]

In addition, the colonel had deeply imprinted García Márquez
with a heightened sense of the importance of politics. The boy
learned how governments can affect the lives of ordinary people,
either for good or for ill. And Nicolás Márquez drilled into his
grandson a liberal, leftist point of view that emphasized a healthy
distrust of powerful politicians and big businesses that get rich
by exploiting the poor.

A Ready-Made Family

The profound influence of García Márquez's grandparents ended
rather abruptly, however, in the mid-1930s, when the boy was
eight. The colonel died of cancer, and Doña Tranquilina rapidly
began losing her eyesight. As a result, García Márquez's parents
decided that he should live with them. His father was planning
to open a pharmacy in Barranquilla, situated on the Caribbean
seacoast about 50 miles (80km) west of Aracataca. By that time,
his parents had had five more children, two boys and three girls,
so García Márquez found himself the eldest of six children.
(Eventually, his parents had five more children, giving the future
novelist a total of ten younger siblings.)

García Márquez had briefly visited his parents on occasion over
the years. But he felt that he did not know them very well and at
times, after months apart, he could not remember clearly what

they looked like. Years later he described his uneasy feelings about his mother during one of these visits:

> I stood petrified in the doorway, not knowing which of [the several women in the room] was my mother until she opened her arms to me. . . . Her embrace surrounded me in the particular scent I always smelled on her, and a lightning flash of guilt shook me body and soul because I knew my duty was to love her but I felt that I did not.[17]

The Most Important Writer

"I believe he's the most important writer of fiction in any language since William Faulkner died."

—Bill Clinton, quoted in "García Márquez Delights Bill Clinton," *North County Times* (San Diego). www.nctimes.com/articles/2007/03/27/news/nation/16_38_263_26_07.txt.

Scared and disconcerted, the boy worried that adjusting to life with a ready-made family of seven people he hardly knew was going to be awkward and difficult. But he was relieved to find his father surprisingly easy to get along with. In fact, García treated his son more as a fellow grownup than as a boy. Also, the father showed that he was a far more worthy individual than his in-laws had made him out to be. Though lacking a formal education, García loved learning and had gained much knowledge by reading books. This proved fortunate for the boy. As time went on, García instilled in his son a love for reading and literature. No one guessed at the time that this love for the written word, coupled with the ghosts and vivid stories of his singular childhood, had put García Márquez on the path to the uncertain life of a writer.

Chapter 2

Finding His Way

The fifteen years from about 1935 to 1950 became the second major formative period of García Márquez's life. Between the ages of eight and twenty-three, he attended a series of schools, became a voracious reader, and learned what it was like to live on his own, away from the watchful eyes of his relatives. These years also witnessed the young man's life-altering decision to pursue a career as a writer and his first struggles to get his works published. In addition, he struggled to find a unique, personal literary voice; this was not easy because he was strongly influenced by a number of great writers and openly copied various aspects of their styles.

Meanwhile, García Márquez could not divorce his interest in writing from the onrush of dramatic political developments. This period of his life turned out to be one of the most violent and chaotic in Colombia's history. And the young man found himself thrust directly into the center of the social strife produced by that turmoil. Along with his memories of his grandfather's stories about past political unrest, the new disorder strongly shaped the settings and themes of his youthful writing.

A Latin American Influence

In addition to American novelists William Faulkner and Ernest Hemingway, a number of Latin American writers influenced García Márquez's writing style and views of the world. Among these Latin Americans was the world-renowned poet Pablo Neruda, whom García Márquez particularly admired. Born in Chile in 1904, Neruda was so talented that he began publishing poems and articles in local newspapers at the age of thirteen. As a young adult, he became a diplomat for the Chilean government, visiting nations across the globe. In 1945, Neruda joined the Communist Party and began fighting for better treatment of miners and other workers. His activism angered government authorities and forced him to go into hiding for two years. As a writer, his most celebrated achievement was *Cantato General*, a collection of more than three hundred poems. In 1971, two years before his death, he won the Nobel Prize for Literature. Like García Márquez, therefore, whose works he greatly enjoyed, Neruda mixed politics with writing and won the most prestigious prize the international community bestows on authors.

Poet Pablo Neruda influenced García Márquez's writing style.

School Days

Many years before he made the formal decision to become a writer, García Márquez struggled diligently to acquire the most elementary of reading and writing skills. Soon after he moved from Aracataca to Barranquilla, his parents enrolled him in a local grade school. He later revealed the difficulty of learning to read and how people marveled at his dedication:

> It did not seem logical for the letter m to be called em, and yet with some vowel following it you did not say ema, but ma. It was impossible for me to read that way. At last, when I went to [school], the teacher did not teach me the names of the consonants but their sounds. In this way I could read the first book I found in a dusty chest in the storeroom of the house. It was tattered and incomplete, but it involved me in so intense a way that [a family friend] had a terrifying premonition as he walked by [me]: "Damn! This kid's going to be a writer!"[18]

It was not long before the boy was writing humorous little poems, which became well known among his classmates and teachers. Still, he was shy rather than outgoing. And his demeanor seemed so serious most of the time that the other students started calling him "the old man."

García Márquez's dedication to his schoolwork and to reading eventually paid off. In 1940, when he was about thirteen, he passed the placement exam for the Lieco Nacional, a prestigious national secondary school. It was located in Zipaquirá, about 30 miles (48km) north of Colombia's capital city, Bogotá, in the country's central highlands. The boy showed so much promise that, to his parents' delight, he also won a scholarship to pay for his room and board.

Away from all his relatives for the first time in his life, García Márquez thought about his new situation and found it a mixed blessing. On the one hand, he disliked Bogotá and its suburbs intensely, finding them dull and soulless. Also, the frequent cool temperatures of the uplands made him uncomfortable, as he had spent his entire life in the country's more tropical coastal region.

On the other hand, the boy was pleased with the school and enjoyed meeting young people from all parts of his culturally diverse nation. He later wrote, "The four years of harmonious coexistence with everyone [in the school] instilled a unitary vision of the nation in me. I discovered how diverse we were and what we were good for, and I learned and never forgot that the entire country was in fact the sum total of each one of us."[19]

Colombian politics was a frequent topic of conversation at the school. Students and teachers alike had their opinions about the government, the liberals, the conservatives, and the ongoing squabbles among members of these parties. A number of García Márquez's teachers were liberals who did not hesitate to offer their personal views to their students, reinforcing the leftist ideas that had been drilled into the boy by his grandfather. Colombian liberals said they wanted to see people of lesser means, who made up the bulk of the population, enjoy more educational and job opportunities and achieve social equality with the rich and powerful. As a result of this ongoing political debate, "when I left [the Lieco Nacional]," he said years later, "I wanted to do something to bring about a more just society."[20]

A New Circle of Friends

It would be a long time, however, before García Márquez would find himself in a position to exert any significant influence on Colombian society. For the moment, he remained an obscure student struggling to find his own way in life. After graduating from the Lieco Nacional in the mid-1940s, he lacked a clear idea of what he should do next. So he caved into pressure from his parents, who strongly urged him to enroll in a well-respected law school in Bogotá.

Before beginning law school, the eighteen-year-old García Márquez took a few months off to visit his parents in Barranquilla. There, he encountered a thirteen-year-old girl he had met a few years before through family friends. Her name was Mercedes Barcha Pardo. Of partial Egyptian descent, she fascinated the young man, who found her attractive, intelligent, and fun to be with. Not long before returning to the capital, he proposed to her. Although she readily accepted his offer, she wanted to finish school before getting married. So they agreed to put off the wedding to some undetermined future date, when both felt the time was right. At that moment, neither could have foreseen that it would be fourteen years before they would finally marry.

Something Original

"I was aware that García Márquez had a habit of making things up during his interviews. He liked to give each journalist a gift, something original, so they didn't go away with the same old stuff."

—Katie Davis, "Meeting Gabriel García Márquez," National Public Radio. www.npr.org/templates/story/story.php?storyId=1495140.

Leaving Mercedes to continue her classes in Barranquilla, García Márquez began his law classes at the university in Bogotá. From the start, he was unable to muster the slightest bit of interest in his studies. He frequently skipped class and spent hours wandering through the capital, eating in cheap cafés and getting to know starving artists and young would-be writers and journalists. The conversations he had with these ardent intellectuals were far more compelling and enlightening than anything he heard in the few law classes he did attend.

The aspiring writers among García Márquez's new circle of friends also reinforced his growing passion for reading and literature. In fact, one day one of them gave him a book that brought about what he later viewed as an important turning point in his life. The book was *The Metamorphosis*, by the renowned Czech writer Franz Kafka. The famous opening line electrified García Márquez: "When Gregor Samsa woke up one morning from unsettling dreams, he found himself changed in his bed into a monstrous vermin."[21] Then, after this audacious, unexpected start, the story unfolds in a matter-of-fact, mostly realistic manner.

The book's first few pages jolted García Márquez into a new awareness of the possibilities of the written word. "I thought to myself," he later recalled, "that I didn't know anyone was allowed to write things like that. If I had known, I would have started writing a long time ago." He now saw that a piece of literature did not have to follow a straight narrative and unfold along a traditional plot. He felt liberated by that thought. García Márquez

García Márquez's early writings were influenced by the Czech author Franz Kafka.

also noticed that Kafka's writing style strongly resembled the tone and delivery of his grandmother's tales. "That's how my grandmother used to tell stories," he remembered, by saying "the wildest things with a completely natural tone of voice."[22]

The First Short Story

Thanks to his introduction to Kafka, García Márquez felt himself drawn to the idea of becoming a writer. Yet this seemed a daunting goal. He felt that he needed to catch up on the many pieces of great literature he had not yet had the chance to read. At the same time, he was inspired to try his hand at writing. The result was his first short story, "The Third Resignation." Its style was very similar to Kafka's, for the young, inexperienced writer had not yet found his own literary voice, but rather, as one critic puts it, "blatantly transferred his reading to what he was writing."[23]

The plot of the story follows a young boy who falls into a coma and whose mother hides his unmoving body in a coffin for eighteen years. In later years, some critics suggested that the claustrophobic qualities of the story are a metaphor for the oppressive rule of a number of South American dictators. Whether or not García Márquez had such a parallel in mind, which is doubtful, there is no doubt that the highly Kafkaesque story was thoroughly unoriginal.

García Márquez always found it difficult to separate his fiction from the political climate of his native Colombia.

Yet "The Third Resignation" was also well crafted and showed that its author possessed promise as a writer. Not surprisingly, therefore, it caught the eye of an editor at a liberal Bogotá newspaper, *El Espectador*. The paper published the story, along with some introductory hype about its author being "the new genius of Colombian letters."[24] Extremely encouraged, García Márquez penned a second story, "Eva Is Inside Her Cat," which the paper published in October 1947, when the author was about twenty. Nine more stories followed in the next few years, all of which were published by local newspapers.

The Violence

Though he had made a small splash as a writer, García Márquez did not yet feel confident enough to pursue writing full-time. He also did not relish the idea of upsetting his parents, who were still pushing him to finish law school. So he struggled along at the university while writing in his spare time.

Then, quite suddenly, the young man's life took another major, unexpected turn. He found himself caught up in one of the most horrific episodes in Colombian history—La Violencia, or "the Violence." The trouble began on April 9, 1948, when a popular liberal politician and candidate for the presidency—Jorge Eliécer Gaitán—was assassinated in the capital. Huge riots erupted as liberals from inside and outside the city clashed with conservatives. García Márquez and many of his literary friends took part in the commotion, in which hundreds of buildings burned and more than 2,500 people died.

The three days of upheaval in the capital turned out to be only a prelude to larger-scale violence. Liberals and conservatives formed guerrilla armies, and a bloody civil war raged for years to come, especially in the region around the capital. Not until the late 1950s did the fighting end, leaving hundreds of thousands of Colombians dead and many others homeless.

After the onset of the Violence, García Márquez did not feel safe in Bogotá. So he moved to the coastal town of Cartagena, south of Barranquilla, which was less dangerous than the capital. He enrolled in the law school of the University of Cartagena and also found a job writing a daily column for a liberal local news-

After fleeing the capital for safety reasons, García Márquez enrolled in law school at the University of Cartagena, housed in a former monastery.

paper, *El Universal*. The column, titled "Period. New Paragraph," presented commentary on both literary and political topics.

Adventures in Barranquilla

García Márquez learned a great deal about writing from the paper's editor in chief, Clemente Manuel Zabala. But the many hours the young man spent at the newspaper office caused him to neglect his law studies. He finally decided that pursuing a law career was a waste of his time. In 1950, he quit law school, a move that greatly disappointed his parents.

Having finally made the decision to devote his life to writing, García Márquez moved once again to Barranquilla. There, he fell in with a group of eager, talented young writers very much like himself. They met at coffee shops or at one another's apartments to talk about their favorite authors, especially those frequently discussed and praised by famous literary critics and publications. What became known as the Barranquilla Group (or more simply the Barranquillas) included, besides García Márquez himself, Alfonso Fuenmayer, Alvaro Cepeda Samudio, Germán Vargas, and the oldest of the group, Ramón Vinyes. As it turned out, none of these writers ever gained the level of fame that García Márquez did, yet at the time their influence and guidance were invaluable. "For me," he later recalled,

The Magdalena River flows by the city of Barranquilla. It was in this city that García Márquez and his friends formed the Barranquilla Group, a society of young writers who met in coffee shops or apartments to discuss literature.

the most important thing about the Barranquilla Group is that I had all sorts of books available. They were voracious readers [and] they all had books. We'd get drunk until sunrise talking about literature, and one night there might be ten books I didn't know, but the next day I had them. Germán would bring me two, Alfonso three. . . . The old man, Ramón Vinyes, would let us get involved in all sorts of reading adventures.[25]

Friends

"The truth is that without the obstinacy of his friends, García Márquez would perhaps still today be an unknown writer."

—Mario Vargas Llosa, quoted in Joan Mellen, *Literary Masters: Gabriel García Márquez*. Detroit: Gale, 2000, p. 26.

While hobnobbing with his literary friends in Barranquilla, García Márquez tried to earn some money by taking a job writing columns for a local newspaper, *El Heraldo*. But the paper did not pay him very much. He later remembered: "They paid me three pesos for a daily commentary and four for an editorial when one of the staff writers was out, but it was barely enough to live on."[26] Hoping to make extra money by publishing a book, the young man finished his first novel. Titled *La Casa*, it was a chronicle of a poor Colombian family that was clearly a thinly veiled version of his own. Although he had great hopes for the book, the first publisher he sent it to rejected it.

Journey into the Past

But García Márquez soon got over the disappointment he felt at being rebuffed, as an unexpected incident involving his mother pushed him in a fruitful new direction. Luisa Iguarán called on him one day. The vivid impression she made on him at that moment stayed with him ever after, prompting him to write in his autobiography:

She was forty-five. Adding up her eleven births, she had spent almost ten years pregnant and at least another ten nursing her children. She had gone gray before

In Faulkner's Country

American novelist William Faulkner has long been one the biggest influences on García Márquez and his writing style. First, as García Márquez himself has noted, the setting of Faulkner's stories—the American Deep South in the early twentieth century—resembled northern Colombia in the same period. Both cultures featured small rural towns inhabited by mixed races and blighted by poverty. In 1961, García Márquez took a bus through the section of the South that Faulkner wrote about and later commented:

> I saw a world very similar to my home town of Aracataca, [which] had the same wooden shacks with roofs made of zinc and tin. In Faulkner's country, I remember seeing the small stores along the roadway with people seated out front with their feet up on railings. There was the same kind of poverty contrasting with great wealth. In some ways, it seemed to me that Faulkner was also a writer of the Caribbean.

In addition, Faulkner sometimes employed a fictional town in his novels and multiple narrators to unfold the plot. García Márquez used both of these devices in his own works.

Quoted in Gene H. Bell-Villada, ed., *Conversations with Gabriel García Márquez.* Jackson: University Press of Mississippi, 2006, p. 99.

her time, [and] her eyes seemed larger and more startled behind her first bifocals [glasses]. . . . Even before she embraced me, she said in her customary, ceremonial way: "I've come to ask you to please go with me to sell the house." She did not have to tell me which one, or where, because for us only one existed in the world, my grandparents' old house in Aracataca, where I'd had the good fortune to be born.[27]

The house was falling into disrepair, his mother said, and it was no longer worth the time and money to keep up. At the time, García Márquez did not realize that this journey into his past in Aracataca would turn out to be crucial to his future. He wrote later, "Neither my mother nor I, of course, could even have imagined that this simple two-day trip would be so decisive. . . .

I [now] know it was the most important of all the decisions I had to make in my career as a writer."[28]

The reason the train trip to García Márquez's hometown was so pivotal was that it strongly reinforced his memories of the singular atmosphere of the place. Its remoteness, poverty, seediness, slow-paced lifestyle, and the feeling that veiled secrets lurked behind every door all flooded back to him. He suddenly realized why *La Casa* did not work, either as a novel or as a basic storyline. It was too generalized and generic; that is, the family and town he described in it could be any one of many in Colombia and Latin America. It struck García Márquez that he needed to

A sign in Aracataca advertises the banana plantation Macondo, which is located there. In his famous work One Hundred Years of Solitude, *García Márquez named the fictionalized version of his hometown "Macondo," after the plantation.*

personalize the story he wanted to tell, to draw on his specific memories of Aracataca, the people who inhabited it, and the house that harbored the ghosts of his grandparents.

He would not call it Aracataca, however, he decided. Instead, he would give it a different name. That way, the real town and its people would infuse a needed authentic quality and local color into his writing, but no one would be able to locate the place he was describing. That would give it an air of mystery—a distant, intriguing, and perhaps mythical quality that a reader could not quite identify.

But what should he call the town? During the train ride, García Márquez noticed an old banana plantation not far from the tracks. A half-fallen, faded sign read: *Macondo*. That name burned into his mind and took up permanent residence there. In the days that followed, as a much revised version of *La Casa* swirled through his head, he realized that the story's setting must be the semi-mythical town of Macondo. At the time, García Márquez had no inkling that several years hence, millions of people around the world would be entranced by his descriptions of that sleepy, decaying little town.

Chapter 3

World Traveler

From the standpoint of sheer physical output and mobility, the period lasting from the early 1950s until the mid-1960s was the busiest and most varied of García Márquez's life. He worked almost constantly as a journalist for several newspapers and other publications. Some of these jobs included assignments that took him out of the country. For several years he traveled widely, visiting, living, and working in numerous countries in Europe and the Americas. These world travels introduced him to foreign political ideas and events that he hoped would be useful in reforming Colombian politics, which remained mired down in the mutual hatreds of local partisan groups.

All the while, García Márquez kept up his writing. In addition to his news articles and commentary, he turned out several works of fiction, in which he continued striving to find his personal literary voice. But in large degree it still lay buried beneath the stylistic influence of famous writers he admired, especially American novelists William Faulkner and Ernest Hemingway.

A Memorable Encounter

García Márquez idolized American novelist Ernest Hemingway and counted himself fortunate that he had a chance encounter with Hemingway on a Paris street in 1957. Looking back in a 2007 online article, García Márquez recalled:

> I recognized him immediately, passing with his wife Mary Welsh on the Boulevard St. Michel in Paris one rainy spring day in 1957. He walked on the other side of the street . . . wearing a very worn pair of cowboy pants, a plaid shirt, and a ball-player's cap. . . . For a fraction of a second [I] found myself divided between my two competing roles. I didn't know whether to ask him for an interview or cross the avenue to express my unqualified admiration for him. . . . So I didn't do either of the things that could have spoiled that moment, but instead cupped both hands over my mouth and, like Tarzan in the jungle, yelled from one sidewalk to the other: "Maaaeeestro!" Ernest Hemingway understood that there could be no other master amid the multitude of students, and he turned, raised his hand and shouted to me in Castilian in a very childish voice, "Adiooos, amigo!" It was the only time I saw him.

Gabriel García Márquez, "Gabriel García Márquez Meets Ernest Hemingway." www.nytimes.com/books/99/07/04/specials/hemingway-marquez.html.

Writing *Leaf Storm*

Faulkner (1897–1962), for instance, was García Márquez's chief influence in revising his failed novel, *La Casa*. The still obscure Colombian writer had long found Faulkner's works compelling. "When I first read Faulkner," he once said, "I thought: I must become a writer."[29] Author of the widely acclaimed novels *The Sound and the Fury* (1929) and *Intruder in the Dust* (1948), Faulkner had won the Nobel Prize for Literature in 1949. A native of Mississippi, he had grown up in a small, rural, largely poor town, just as García Márquez had. And Faulkner had set some of his works in a fictional southern town based closely on the town of his birth.

Giving his first novel a new title—*Leaf Storm*—García Márquez employed the same approach, calling the fictionalized version of his own hometown *Macondo*. He also sought to create the same oppressive atmosphere of poverty, social backwardness, and general hopelessness that characterized Faulkner's setting. The action of *Leaf Storm* takes place in Macondo between 1903 and 1928. As in the real Aracataca, the inhabitants of Macondo are poor and downtrodden until a foreign banana company ushers in a period of boom and prosperity. But then the company pulls out, leaving the town to decline back into poverty and decadence. These events are told by three narrators—a young boy, who resembles García Márquez as a child; the boy's mother, who has much in common

García Márquez's novel Leaf Storm *was heavily influenced by the writings of the American author William Faulkner (pictured).*

with the author's mother, Luisa; and the boy's grandfather, a character based on García Márquez's own grandfather, the colonel.

In a way, as in García Márquez's later books set in Macondo, the town itself is a sort of character. "It is indeed the community," Ruben Pelayo points out, that the narrators

> call "the leaf storm," which supplies the story's title. Unlike single characters developed in a detailed way, the community as character can be better understood if the reader thinks of it as atmosphere. The community as character can be seen through the mood, the feelings, the interpersonal relations among the townspeople, and the relationships between the townspeople and their institutions. Macondo thus becomes a physical place, although imaginary, in the minds of the readers.[30]

Publication of *Leaf Storm*

García Márquez completed *Leaf Storm* in 1952. At first, he was enthusiastic, believing that the much improved manuscript would be far better received than *La Casa* had been. However, the publisher he sent it to rejected it. Gripped by self-doubt, García Márquez tossed the manuscript into a desk drawer, unsure if he would ever look at or deal with it again.

Light on His Feet

"He is stocky, but light on his feet, with a bristling mustache, a cauliflower nose, and many fillings in his teeth. He wears an open sport shirt, faded blue jeans, and a bulky jacket flung over his shoulders."

—Luis Harss, quoted in "Gabriel García Márquez, or the Lost Chord," in Luis Harss and Barbara Dohmann, *Into the Mainstream: Conversations with Latin-American Writers*. New York: Harper and Row, 1967, p. 310.

Fortunately for the reading public, this was not the end of the novel. Two years later, when García Márquez was out of the country on a journalistic assignment, some friends of his from the Barranquilla Group secretly removed the manuscript from the drawer. They offered the book to a different publisher, who accepted it and printed it in 1955. *Leaf Storm* sold several thousand copies in Colombia, but it made no significant impact beyond the author's homeland, and all involved, especially García Márquez, were disappointed that it did not do better.

When the book first appeared, there were very few critical evaluations by widely respected literary authorities. Later critics, writing after García Márquez had become a world-class author, noted that *Leaf Storm* contains a number of thematic elements, settings, and character types that he used later in his masterpiece, *One Hundred Years of Solitude*. The general view seems to be that the earlier work is an immature precursor of the later one. Critic Luis Harss, who interviewed García Márquez on several occasions in the 1960s, said, "On the whole, one can say that a lot of energy goes to waste in *Leaf Storm*, which for all its genuine emotional charge remains shapeless and diffuse."[31] García Márquez himself later suggested that his youthful enthusiasm for and conscious imitation of Faulkner and other famous writers was responsible for the book's shortcomings:

> I've a great deal of affection for *Leaf Storm*. Even lots of compassion for that guy who wrote it. I can see him perfectly. A twenty-two or twenty-three-year-old kid who feels that he's not going to write anything else in life, feels it's his only chance, and he tries to throw in everything he remembers, everything he's learned about literary technique and sophistication from every author he's seen.[32]

To Europe and Back

The writing and publication of *Leaf Storm* took place during a period when García Márquez, then in his early twenties, was growing restless. He had spent his entire life in northern and central Colombia. He longed to see more of his native country and to travel to other lands, including the United States and Europe, which had produced many of his favorite writers. At first, his travels were rather modest. In 1953 he took a job as an encyclopedia salesman and knocked on doors in a number of Colombian towns he had never visited before. That same year he and Mercedes, then nineteen, got engaged. They still did not set a firm

When he moved back to Bogotá, García Márquez obtained a job writing for the newspaper, El Espectador. *The newspaper was housed in this building.*

date for their marriage, but they agreed that they would remain true to each other until that day came.

Quickly bored with the encyclopedia job, in 1954 García Márquez moved back to Bogotá, where the level of violence had significantly declined in recent months. There, he landed a job with *El Espectador*, the newspaper that had published his first short stories. Promising to print more of the young author's stories, the managing editor also asked García Márquez to write regular film reviews for the paper. García Márquez, a staunch movie fan, happily accepted this assignment, which marked the beginning of many film-related projects he would tackle in his long career, including writing screenplays.

García Márquez had been working for *El Espectador* for only a few months when his boss offered him what all the reporters at the paper viewed as a choice assignment. Pope Pius XII, supreme leader of the world's Roman Catholics, including those in Colombia, was very ill and supposedly near death. García Márquez's job was to travel to Italy to cover the pontiff's passing. As it turned out, the pope did not die as expected. But García Márquez remained in Europe for several months, penning news and human interest stories and sending them back to the paper in Bogotá. It was during this period that his writer friends rescued the manuscript of *Leaf Storm* and got it published.

Like a Flock of Parrots

"Reading Gabriel García Márquez is like watching a flock of parrots. They're colorful. They fly. They speak to you. Except that these birds tell you things you'd never expect."

—Douglas Lawson, "Strange Pilgrims."
http://ebbs.english.vt.edu/olp/gs/1.1/marquez.html.

Returning to Colombia in 1955, García Márquez hoped that he would achieve at least a modest amount of fame for his recently published novel. Instead, he gained considerable public recognition for a news story rather than his fiction. The dramatic series of events began with the near sinking of a Colombian warship, the *Caldas*, in the sea near Cartagena. Though a number of sailors died, one, Luis Alejandro Velasco, survived and became an instant national hero. But Velasco felt guilty because he knew that the *Caldas* had been carrying illegal cargo and that the sailors had died because of the negligence of the ship's officers. He decided to tell the truth about what had happened to *El Espectador*, and García Márquez was chosen to interview him and write the lead story.

The article, titled "The Truth About My Adventure, by Luis Alejandro Velasco," was widely read by the Colombian public and raised a huge controversy. Embarrassed because it had taken part in the cover-up of the fiasco, the government kicked Velasco out of the navy. The editors of *El Espectador* worried that the authorities' wrath might next fall on García Márquez. So they sent him on assignment to Europe once more, figuring they could bring him back when the commotion surrounding the *Caldas* incident had subsided.

Thrilled to be back in Europe, García Márquez wandered from country to country. He visited Switzerland, Poland, and Hungary and then went to France. In Paris, a city that enthralled him, he was shocked to learn that the Colombian government had closed down *El Espectador*, seeing it as too subversive. Dependent on the small salary his boss had been forwarding him, García Márquez now found himself stranded in Europe with no way to get home.

Two New Books

Desperate, García Márquez managed to subsist on the little he could make from the deposits on empty bottles he collected along the roadside. Then he had a stroke of luck. The kindly manager of his hotel took pity on his situation and allowed him to live there on credit. (She never tried to collect the debt.)

Marooned in Europe, the young man decided to put the time to good use. He worked furiously, sometimes day and night, on two new novels. In fact, he labored so hard that his typewriter broke down and he had to take it to a repair shop. There, the repairman told him in a sympathetic voice, "It is exhausted, sir."[33]

The first of the two novels is titled *No One Writes to the Colonel*. It is set in a backward little town very similar to his hometown of Aracataca, though it is not Macondo; rather, the author describes the unnamed village as lying several miles downstream from Macondo. The title character, the colonel, based on his grandfather, is a former soldier who now lives in abject poverty, waiting endlessly for government pension checks that have been promised but never actually appear.

Whereas García Márquez's first novel, *Leaf Storm*, had displayed the profound influence of Faulkner, *No One Writes to the Colonel* owed much to Hemingway (1899–1961). Author of *For Whom the Bell Tolls* (1940) and *The Old Man and the Sea* (1952), Hemingway won the Nobel Prize in 1954. The younger writer felt a strong affinity for Hemingway's work habits and practical approach to writing. Years later, García Márquez said:

García Márquez adopted many of the techniques and the sparse writing style of the American author Ernest Hemingway (pictured).

Faulkner is a writer who has had much to do with my soul, but Hemingway is the one who had the most to do with my craft, not simply for his books, but for his astounding knowledge of the aspect of craftsmanship in the science of writing. . . . [He said] that when writing becomes hard it is good to reread one's own books, in order to remember that it always was hard; that one can write anywhere so long as there are no visitors and no telephone. [Finally] his lesson was the discovery that each day's work should only be interrupted when one knows where to begin again the next day. I don't think that any more useful advice has ever been given about writing.[34]

García Márquez was also inspired by Hemingway's writing style. He liked the way that the famous author adopted a relatively simple theme or plot, one suitable for a short story, and stretched it into a novel. He also admired and adopted Hemingway's tendency to refrain from explaining certain things, thereby leaving the reader guessing. "His novels are like short stories that are out of proportion, that include too much," García Márquez later recalled. "In contrast, the best thing about his stories is that they give the impression something is missing, and this is precisely what confers their mystery and their beauty."[35]

The second work García Márquez completed during his European sojourn was a novella (short novel) titled *In Evil Hour*. The story takes place in the same unnamed village in which *No One Writes to the Colonel* is set, and many of the same characters appear. This time, however, the mood is darker. An unknown person has been plastering the town with posters containing scandalous gossip about various townspeople. In their search for the

Suspense Without Resolution

Setting his story in a fictional town, giving that town an oppressive atmosphere, and injecting touches of the supernatural are not the only hallmarks of the style García Márquez brought to maturity in *One Hundred Years of Solitude*. He also employs an unusual literary device that can frustrate readers, yet makes them want to read on. He accomplishes this by building up a considerable amount of suspense and then leaving out a concrete resolution. "After the build-up," a noted literary critic suggests, "any resolution would seem pedestrian [commonplace]," so García Márquez avoids it:

He likes to take the reader to the edge of the obvious, then drop him, leaving him in suspense. This method is not always successful. Indeed, it can be irritating. But it adds to the ominous atmosphere. And after the book is shut and put away, that is what remains. Macondo is an anguished town in the throes of dark [destiny]: senseless wars, general pestilence, and decay. The mood is epidemic.

Luis Harss, "Gabriel García Márquez, or the Lost Chord," in Luis Harss and Barbara Dohmann, *Into the Mainstream: Conversations with Latin-American Writers.* New York: Harper and Row, 1967, p. 324.

culprit, the authorities resort to repressive measures that turn the citizens against one another, a clear echo of the civil strife in the author's own homeland in recent years.

Venezuela, Cuba, New York, and Mexico

Parts of *In Evil Hour* were written after García Márquez left Paris. Resuming his travels, he went first to London and then managed to scrape together enough money to return to South America. But he stayed away from Colombia, realizing he was still unwelcome there. He settled instead in neighboring Venezuela, where in 1957 he began working for a liberal weekly newspaper, *Elite*. The managing editor, Plinio Apuleyo Mendoza, a leftist, was a political kindred spirit who wanted to see Colombia's corrupt government reformed. Once again, García Márquez found himself in Europe, as the two men, subsidized by the newspaper, toured the Communist countries of Eastern Europe. They hoped to find political solutions there that could be transferred to Latin America. But they were sorely disappointed. It quickly became clear that European communism was just as repressive as the broken political system in Colombia.

Not long after the two men returned to Venezuela, García Márquez decided to go back to Barranquilla. He missed Mercedes and thought it unfair to keep her waiting for him year after year. They were finally married in 1958. But it was clear that it would be unsafe for them to remain in Colombia, so they slipped away and found a place to stay in Venezuela's capital, Caracas.

The move proved only temporary, however. The following year, the couple moved to Havana, Cuba, so García Márquez could see firsthand and write about the ongoing Communist revolution there. The leftist rebel Fidel Castro was consolidating his gains in his successful fight against Cuba's corrupt traditional government. García Márquez sympathized with the revolutionaries, seeing parallels between their struggle and the need for political reforms in his own country.

While they were in Cuba, their first son, Rodrigo, was born. The family might well have stayed on the island had it not been for a new opportunity that allowed García Márquez to combine

Soon after García Márquez married Mercedes Barcha Pardo, in 1958, they relocated to Venezuela. Here the couple is pictured in their later years.

his interests in writing and politics. On behalf of the Cuban government, he moved his family to New York City. There he ran the North American branch of the Cuban news agency, Prensa Latina. After a year, however, he resigned and the family moved again, this time to Mexico City, where he worked on several screenplays that did not sell. It was there, in 1962, that he and his wife had their second son, Gonzalo.

Exhausted by his years of traveling and preoccupied with taking care of his family, García Márquez now entered what he later described as a lean time in his writing career. This period was so lacking in literary inspiration that he did not imagine he would ever become an important or well-known writer. As Raymond Williams puts it:

His writing had exerted virtually no impact outside Colombia and relatively little in his homeland, beyond the group of intellectuals and friends who read his novels. . . . Even García Márquez himself was not planning to write any more fiction after 1962. The years from 1962 to 1965 were not only devoid of literary publications, but also barren of serious fictional creation.[36]

Unbeknownst to García Márquez and those who knew him, this dry spell in his literary output was simply another of the many temporary phases in his life. Sudden inspiration would soon combine with his latent talent and some good old-fashioned hard work to produce a masterpiece.

Chapter 4

Breakthrough and Fame

The year was 1965, and García Márquez was about thirty-eight years old. As he and his wife were driving from Mexico City to Acapulco, where they had planned to spend a quiet vacation, the great breakthrough of his life occurred. In a jolting epiphany, he at last realized how to express his personal literary voice. Though he had suffered from near writer's block for almost three years, the shape of a new novel rapidly took form in his mind. "All of a sudden," he later recalled, "I don't know why, [but] I had this illumination on how to write the book." In fact, "I had it so completely formed, that right there I could have dictated the first chapter word by word to a typist."[37]

Having been struck by a proverbial lightning bolt of inspiration, García Márquez cried out to his wife that they must turn around and go back to their house in Mexico City. He needed to begin writing a new novel immediately, he explained. When they reached the house, this single-minded goal took complete possession of him. He informed Mercedes that, like Hemingway, he must be allowed to work in total isolation, with no interruptions that might break his train of thought. In the meantime, she would have to take care of the house and children and all family matters. It might take up to six months to finish the work, he warned, half a year in which he would be effectively out of touch with the family and the world.

Mercedes, who had already proven herself a dutiful and patient partner, said that she understood. She promised to support him 100 percent, to grant him the quiet and privacy he required, to keep him supplied with paper and other essentials, and when necessary to bring him his meals. Then she watched him retreat into his office-study. As she would learn in the months that followed, he would only rarely and briefly emerge from its confines before completing his masterpiece, *One Hundred Years of Solitude*.

The crowded Mexico City skyline is pictured on a rare smog-free day. While en route to Acapulco for vacation, García Márquez became so inspired to write his next book that he insisted on returning home to Mexico City immediately.

A Place Everywhere and Nowhere

As for what exactly had sparked this sudden literary revelation, García Márquez himself could not say for sure. What was certain to him was that the sum total of his memories and life experiences had unexpectedly come together and pointed him in a certain direction. For reasons that he could not put into words, he instinctively knew that it was for him the *right* direction. He was sure that if he followed his instincts, his unique tone of voice as a novelist would be unleashed.

These instincts seemed to flow from a place deep inside him, where his childhood experiences and early impressions of the world resided. "The tone that I eventually used in *One Hundred Years of Solitude* was based on the way my grandmother used to tell stories," he later wrote.

> She told things that sounded supernatural and fantastic, but she told them with complete naturalness. . . . What was most important was the expression she had on her face. She did not change her expression at all when telling her stories and everyone was surprised. In previous attempts to write, I tried to tell the story without believing in it. I discovered that what I had to do was believe in them myself and write them with the same expression with which my grandmother told them—with a brick face.[38]

García Márquez also realized that the atmosphere of his childhood was as important to the new novel as his tone of voice in writing it. He knew that he must set the events of the story in a town very much like his native Aracataca. His first novel, *Leaf Storm*, had used this approach. In that book, the real Aracataca had been transformed into the fictional Macondo. Yet García Márquez now felt that the characters and events of *Leaf Storm* had been mere precursors, little more than a prelude to a much larger and more dramatic exploration of Macondo and its troubles.

As it had been in *Leaf Storm*, Macondo became in a sense the central character in *One Hundred Years of Solitude*. García Márquez knew that if he could make his readers accept the town's reality and visualize it vividly, they would inevitably be drawn into the

The Origin of Macondo

In the first installment of his autobiography, published in 2003, García Márquez tells how he found the name *Macondo*, which he used for a fictional town in some of his novels, while riding on a train toward his hometown of Aracataca.

The train stopped at a station that had no town, and a short while later it passed the only banana plantation along the route that had its name written over the gate: *Macondo*. This word had attracted my attention ever since the first trips I had made with my grandfather, but I discovered only as an adult that I liked its poetic resonance. I never heard anyone say it and did not even ask myself what it meant. I had already used it in three books as the name of an imaginary town when I happened to read in an encyclopedia that it is a tropical tree resembling the ceiba, that it produces no flowers or fruit, and that its light, porous wood is used for making canoes.

Gabriel García Márquez, *Living to Tell the Tale*, trans. Edith Grossman. New York: Knopf, 2003, p. 19.

García Márquez and his wife, Mercedes, travel by train to Aracataca in 2007. It was on a similar journey that García Márquez came up with the name "Macondo."

complex, powerful tale of its rise and fall. Therefore, making Macondo seem to be a real place became his initial goal in the writing process. The scope of this accomplishment becomes clear when one considers that Macondo is "not on any map," as one modern expert points out:

> Macondo, set between dunes and marshlands on one side and an impenetrable sierra on another, is a decadent, dusty little coastal town, like thousands of others in the heart of the hemisphere, but also very special, at once strange and familiar, specific and general, immediate as an insight, remote as an image of forgotten landscape. It is one of those places a voyager reaches without ever leaving home. Macondo is everywhere and nowhere. Those who travel there take an inner trip to a port of call that is part of the hidden face of a country.[39]

Almost Biblical

"I have just finished reading *One Hundred Years of Solitude* [in which] Macondo is made into a universal territory, in a story almost biblical in its foundations."

—Carlos Fuentes, quoted in Joan Mellen, *Literary Masters: Gabriel García Márquez*. Detroit: Gale, 2000, p. 49.

There is a reason that Macondo's face is hidden from humanity's mainstream, a reason that García Márquez reveals as he unfolds the book's plot. It is a rundown, unattractive place in part because of natural decay. Macondo, like so many real-life South American towns in the nineteenth and early twentieth centuries, has been plagued by disease epidemics, bandits, droughts, and flash floods. But these turn out to be only the visible, surface drawbacks of the town. Lurking beneath this surface, Luis Harss writes, is a "moral gangrene," a rot that is eating away at the fabric of the local society.

> It is a town of guilty consciences, with a grudge against the world. The past was buried without being exorcised [ridding itself of its sins and guilt], and is back, a dark ferment that has become a collective nightmare. No one

sleeps well in Macondo. There is an atmosphere of distrust and suspicion, repressed violence and hostility. . . . For those who can read the signs, every minute is weighted with a threat of imminent disaster.[40]

Macondo's Rise and Fall

Choosing to set the events of the novel in dusty, decaying Macondo was only the beginning of García Márquez's great vision for the work. He also saw that the plot, or story line, should encompass the events that he knew best and that touched his mind and heart the most; otherwise, the tone of voice of the novel would not be truly and uniquely his. Thus, he must include many of the real events that northern Colombia, his hometown of Aracataca, and his grandparents and parents had witnessed or endured.

Yet at the same time, he planned to frame these events within a larger context. That frame would incorporate and explore certain universal truths and inevitabilities of life and the human condition, such as war, ambition, and family loyalty. Others that his instinct told him he must include were betrayal, sexual passion, belief in the supernatural, decay, natural calamity, and death.

Required Reading

"[*One Hundred Years of Solitude*] is the first piece of literature since the Book of Genesis that should be required reading for the entire human race."

—William Kennedy, quoted in Joan Mellen, *Literary Masters: Gabriel García Márquez*. Detroit: Gale, 2000, p. 49.

With this monumental framework in mind, García Márquez opened the book with what is now viewed as one of the most famous lines in literature: "Many years later, as he faced the firing squad, Colonel Aureliano Buendía was to remember that distant afternoon when his father took him to discover ice."[41] In this one sentence, a tour de force that sets the tone for the rest of the story, the author presents the reader with a triple time frame. First, there is the present, whenever that may be. Then there is the future, represented by the words "many years later." There is also

Pedestrians in Aracataca step over fallen tropical flowers in the city's streets. Aracataca, the small, decaying town, renamed "Macondo," figures prominently in García Márquez's novel, One Hundred Years of Solitude.

the past, when, on a "distant afternoon," the colonel's father took him to see ice. The reader is not only unsure of the time period in which the action begins, but is also introduced to a dizzying series of jumps from one period to another. "Both here and throughout the novel," Raymond Williams points out, "time takes on a certain magical quality that is impossible for the reader to explain totally in rational terms."[42]

It turns out that the colonel mentioned in the opening line is an important member of Macondo's leading family, the Buendías, and leader of the local liberal party. Long before his birth, the author reveals, Macondo had not been politically divided between liberals and conservatives. For an unknown number of years the town had had no significant contact with the outside world, except for a few itinerant gypsies who introduced strange new items, among them ice. But in time, Macondo established contact with neighboring towns. And rivalries developed, which led to political divisions, hatreds, and wars. During the turmoil, various men governed Macondo, some of them corrupt and some of whom died by violence.

Eventually, as García Márquez tells it, a foreign fruit company appears in the area and begins exploiting the local workers. When they go on strike, thousands are massacred by soldiers sent by the authorities. Even worse, it is not the soldiers who are punished for these misdeeds, but the townspeople. After the soldiers dump the bodies into the sea, it begins to rain and the downpour lasts for five years, sending Macondo into decline. In the end, the last of the Buendías finds and translates an ancient prophecy. It had predicted, with uncanny foresight, the inevitable rise and fall of the town, which now disintegrates into nothingness.

From beginning to end, the turbulent story re-creates real events that the young García Márquez heard about from his grandfather and characters eerily similar to people he knew as a child. For instance, there is the memorable episode in which the little boy sees ice for the first time. Also included are the coming of the foreign fruit company, the exploitation of the workers, the strike, and the massacre. All these real events are intertwined with fabricated ones in a morality tale featuring human frailty, violence, and divine retribution on a truly biblical scale.

Beyond the Rules of the Real World

As García Márquez's epic tale of violence, greed, punishment, and death in Macondo spilled out onto paper, outside the study Mercedes struggled to keep the household together. At first, she made do with whatever money they had on hand. But these limited funds quickly ran out and she sold the family car to raise more. As time passed and her husband appeared to be far from finished with his Herculean task, she turned to selling the kitchen appliances to keep him in paper and typewriter ribbons, as well as to pay the bills. Meanwhile, the six months García Márquez had predicted expired. He told his wife that he had only begun to work and that she must expect many more months of the same.

Then something seemingly miraculous happened that helped Mercedes fulfill the promise she had made to give her husband everything he needed to accomplish his great task. At first the immediate neighbors, and then the whole neighborhood, became aware of the family's plight. Perhaps sensing that something remarkable was afoot, people expressed a collective and in some ways inexplicable faith in García Márquez and his project. Housewives began lending Mercedes the appliances she needed. Storekeepers extended the family credit. And many of the people the family owed money to forgave the debts.

While the Mexican community came together to support a fellow Latin American, eight months stretched into ten months and ten months became a year. And still García Márquez was not finished with his book. Mercedes naturally wondered why it was taking her husband so long to finish the novel. After all, none of his earlier books had taken longer than a few months. At the time, she did not realize that behind the closed door of García Márquez's study, he was doing more than simply writing new words. He was also continually reading over what he had already written and adding or arranging material in more appropriate ways. In addition, the manner in which his story was unfolding was complex and supported at every turn by thoughtful and effective literary devices.

An Unreadable Book

"The book is so in love with its own cleverness that it is profoundly unreadable."

—Jonathan Bate, quoted in "Millennium Reputations: Which are the Most Overrated Authors, or Books, of the Past 1,000 Years?" www.themodernword.com/gabo/review_OHYS_bate.html.

One of these devices was the compelling way that García Márquez incorporated the element of myth into what was on the surface a modern, realistic tale. The Colombia of his youth had been awash in local myths. They were not myths in the sense of fabricated, fantastic stories; rather, they were emotionally colored, sometimes exaggerated memories of real events, including the struggles of the common people against more powerful natural and political forces. "I realized that reality is also the myths of the common people," García Márquez later wrote.

It is the beliefs, their legends. They are their everyday life and they affect their triumphs and failures. I realized that reality isn't just the police that kill people, but also everything that forms part of the life of the common people. All of this must be incorporated [into my stories].[43]

This merging of myth and reality, which came to be known as "magical realism," had been inspired by García Márquez's grandmother. "She was a fabulous storyteller," he later wrote,

> who told wild tales of the supernatural with a most solemn expression on her face. As I was growing up, I often wondered whether or not her stories were truthful. Usually I tended to believe her because of her serious, deadpan facial expression. Now, as a writer I do the same thing. I say extraordinary things in a serious

While writing his novel One Hundred Years of Solitude, *García Márquez isolated himself in his study for months to write without being interrupted.*

In 2007, García Márquez holds aloft a special edition of One Hundred Years of Solitude. *The book is a masterwork of time manipulation, simultaneously weaving together the past, present, and future of the book's inhabitants.*

tone. It's possible to get away with *anything* as long as you make it believable. That is something my grand-mother taught me.[44]

Examples of magical realism abound in *One Hundred Years of Solitude*. Gypsies fly on magic carpets and a priest floats in the air when he consumes chocolate. In one arresting scene, a character named Jose Arcadio is shot in the head and the resulting blood flows into the street. The blood takes a twisting, seemingly impossible path until it reaches the feet of Arcadio's grandmother. Observing these and other examples of magical realism, one expert notes, "the reader is dipped slowly into this folk-tale world" of the bleak town of Macondo, where things are not quite the same as they are in the "real" world the reader inhabits. "Macondo works not by the rules that the real world does, but rather by rules that seem almost to make more sense than those of reality. In this way, Macondo works the way we would like to think our world works."[45]

Financial and Critical Success

In a way, the supernormal world of Macondo was paralleled by the artificial little world that García Márquez had created for himself in his study, a miniature universe inhabited only by himself and his fictional characters. His friends had come jokingly to call that stuffy, silent cubicle "the cave of the Mafia." Outside of it, the undeniable reality of a wife, children, friends, and a waiting reading public swirled and beckoned. And finally, after eighteen months—three times longer than he had expected—the tired Colombian emerged, almost like a butterfly from its cocoon. He was holding a thirteen-hundred-page manuscript.

Profoundly Unreadable?

Though many people see *One Hundred Years of Solitude* as a literary classic, not all reviewers and literary critics have liked the book. Jonathan Bate, of the *Sunday Telegraph*, wrote in 1999 that calling the novel great literature "is the most ludicrous gesture of literary hype I have ever encountered":

> The book is so in love with its own cleverness that it is profoundly unreadable. It is generally credited with inaugurating the genre of "magic realism" novels which combine the matter-of-fact narrative style of conventional realistic fiction with fantastic nonsense such as levitation and alchemy. García Márquez is at his most characteristic when a woman ascends to heaven whilst hanging her washing out on the line. Other ingredients of magic realism include gypsies, tarts with hearts, dwarves, tricksters and a cast so large and confusing that you need a family tree to keep track of the plot. Márquez and his followers are sophisticated urban intellectuals who feign reverence for the simple wisdom of peasants. . . . Let us hope that *One Hundred Years of Solitude* will not generate one hundred years of overwritten, overlong, overrated novels.

Jonathan Bate, "Millennium Reputations: Which Are the Most Overrated Authors or Books of the Past 1,000 Years?" www.themodernword.com/gabo/review_OHYS _bate.html.

Mercedes and the others who greeted the longtime hermit were naturally excited that the book was finished and looked forward to its publication. The family was so penniless that García Márquez had to pawn some garden tools to raise the postage to send the manuscript to a publisher. That major publisher—Editorial Sudamericana, in Buenos Aires, Argentina—immediately and eagerly accepted the work and ordered the first print run in June 1967. All eight thousand copies sold out in a single week. This scenario was repeated over and over again, until, at the end of three years, half a million copies had sold. Translations into nearly thirty other languages followed, driving sales even higher. (By 2007, more than 20 million copies of the book had sold.)

Meanwhile, critics across the world raved about *One Hundred Years of Solitude*. The novel won numerous awards, including the prestigious Italian Chianchiano Prize. After decades of obscurity, poverty, and uncertainty, García Márquez had finally found his voice and attained worldwide respect and fame in his chosen profession. He and his wife were also pleased by an added bonus, namely the considerable income the book earned, which made them financially comfortable. Never again, they noted with relief, would they have to sell their belongings to pay for food or postage.

Chapter 5

Political Activist

T he success of *One Hundred Years of Solitude* in the late 1960s and early 1970s brought García Márquez worldwide public recognition and allowed him and his wife and children to enjoy a very comfortable lifestyle. In this period and the years that followed, he continued to turn out new short stories and novels, all of which were published and most of which made handsome profits. In addition, all his earlier works, including *Leaf Storm* and *No One Writes to the Colonel*, were republished, reaching many new readers and making money.

However, literary fame and financial security were not the only benefits that came with García Márquez's newfound success. As he entered his forties, he happily realized that he could now express his personal political views to a far larger audience than had been possible in the past. As Allen Ruch points out:

> Now a famous writer, he was becoming more aware of his own political power, and his increased clout and financial security enabled him to pursue his interests in political activism. [Accordingly, in the 1970s he] stepped up his personal campaign to influence the

world around him, [including funneling] some of his money into political and social causes.[46]

Making monetary donations was not the only way that García Márquez supported various political ideas and causes. He also wrote articles and other short tracts advocating the rights of poor people and laborers in Colombia, Venezuela, Nicaragua, Argentina, and Angola. In addition, he helped establish HABEAS, a political action group that worked to free political prisoners jailed by repressive regimes. And he became friendly with Cuban leader Fidel Castro, whom he had briefly met years before while covering Cuban politics.

As a result of his success, García Márquez felt that he could voice his political views and openly support the causes he believed in.

The causes that García Márquez supported were uniformly liberal or leftist. His grandfather's liberalism, the victimization of Colombian workers in the early twentieth century, and the long feud between right-wing and left-wing parties in his native land had all left an indelible stamp on his psyche. He made no apologies for consistently championing the rights of the poor and underprivileged against rich and powerful individuals, companies, and governments. At times, he even supported Communist activities and revolutions that he felt would aid the poor and powerless. Yet he has repeatedly emphasized that he has never been a member of a Communist party or organization, saying on one occasion:

> I am not and have never been [a Communist]. Nor have I belonged to *any* political party. Sometimes I have the impression that in the United States there is a tendency to separate my writing from my political activities— as if they were opposites. I don't think they are. What happens is that, as an anti-colonial Latin American, I take a position that annoys many interests in the United States. And so, simplistically, some people say that I am an enemy of the United States. What I'd like to correct is the problems and errors in the Americas as a whole. I would think the same way if I were a North American. Indeed, if I *were* North American, I would be even more of a radical, because it would be a matter of correcting the faults of my own country.[47]

The Cuban Revolution

García Márquez's political activities had started in a fairly small way back in 1948, when he took part in the riots in Bogotá that marked the beginning of the period known as the Violence. At the time, he was, from the Colombian government's point of view, only one of many nameless faces in a vast crowd of protesters. But the government got to know him on a more personal basis in 1955, when he interviewed Luis Velasco, the sailor who had survived the near sinking of the warship *Caldas*. Fear of retaliation by the authorities had motivated the writer's boss to send him to Europe, marking the start of his adventures as a world traveler.

Larger-scale political activism began for García Márquez in 1959, when he began reporting on and offering his support for the Cuban Revolution. Three years before, Communist rebel leader Fidel Castro had instigated a guerrilla war against Cuba's authoritarian ruler, Fulgencio Batista. The insurrection achieved success in 1959 and, as a stunned world looked on, Castro took charge of the government. For the first time, a Communist regime had come to power in the Western Hemisphere.

García Márquez, then working for a Venezuelan newspaper, was one of the first Latin American reporters to travel to Cuba's capital, Havana, to cover the Communist takeover. At first, he was sympathetic to the goals of the revolution because Castro had promised to help the island's poor and working classes. García Márquez's work for Prensa Latina, Castro's newly formed news agency, took him to New York City in 1961.

Living and working in the United States was sometimes tense and uncomfortable for the writer. In large part this was because the U.S. government, and Americans in general, did not approve of the rise of communism in Cuba. The depth of anti-Castro feeling in the United States was well illustrated by a controversial event that occurred in that same year. In what came to be called the Bay of Pigs invasion, a group of Cuban exiles who had been trained by the U.S. military tried to attack Cuba, their goal to unseat Castro. The coup failed miserably, greatly embarrassing the U.S. president, John F. Kennedy. García Márquez was openly critical of the invasion and the role the United States had played in it. As a result, he received a number of angry letters, and even a few death threats, from irate Americans. After he left New York for Mexico later in 1961, the U.S. government put him on a blacklist of so-called undesirables who were banned from entering the United States.

Friendship with Castro

After the Bay of Pigs fiasco, Castro became increasingly defensive and cracked down on Cubans who dissented against his regime. He seized control of newspapers, jailed dissidents, and began censoring writers and artists so that they could not criticize his policies. García Márquez, who had always been a staunch supporter

García Márquez (left) supported the ideals of the Cuban Revolution and eventually became good friends with Fidel Castro (right). The two are pictured in Cuba in 1982.

of free speech, protested by resigning his position at Prensa Latina. Nevertheless, he still viewed the Cuban leader as a well-meaning force for good in Latin America. The two became close friends in the 1970s. In praise of Castro, García Márquez wrote:

> His rarest virtue as a politician is the ability to discern how an event will evolve all the way to its farthest consequences, . . . but he practices such ability, not by flashes of inspiration, but as a result of arduous, tenacious reasoning. His supreme assistant is a memory he uses and abuses to back up a speech or a private talk with overwhelming statements and incredibly fast mathematical calculations. . . . When interviewed, usually for hours on end, he dwells on every subject, venturing into its least expected twists and turns without ever neglecting accuracy, aware that a single misused word can bring about irreparable damage. He has never refused to answer any question, nor has he lost patience.[48]

Because of his support for the leftist ideals of the Cuban Revolution, which García Márquez thinks are, at least in theory, fair and just, the writer was criticized by Western journalists and politicians, especially in the United States, for cozying up to a dictator. But he insisted that his friendship with the Cuban leader was on the whole not political. Instead, García Márquez said, he and Castro spent most of their time together discussing literature. "Very few of our conversations concern the fate of the world," the writer has said.

> More often, we talk about what good books we've read. Whenever I go to Cuba, I always take Fidel a stack of books. . . . Once, I remember, I left him a copy of Bram Stoker's *Dracula*, which is really an absolutely fantastic book. . . . "Gabriel, you screwed me!" he [later] said. "That book! I couldn't get a minute's sleep!" He'd read *Dracula* from four in the morning till 11 a.m., and this is an aspect of his personality that few people know.[49]

An Unorthodox Storyteller

"Though widely seen as a political activist of the left, to his friends he is simply unorthodox, a storyteller who objects to theorizing and generalizations."

—Marlise Simmons, quoted in Gene H. Bell-Villada, ed., *Conversations with Gabriel García Márquez*. Jackson: University Press of Mississippi, 2006, p. 154.

Castro has confirmed that his relationship with García Márquez is mainly literary in nature: "I have always received from Gabo pages that he is still working on, with that generous and simple gesture with which he always sent me—and other people whom he appreciates very much—the preliminary drafts of his books, as proof of our old and affectionate friendship."[50]

Fashioning a Dictator

In contrast to the leftist Castro, García Márquez's view of what constitutes a dangerous dictator was shaped by a series of right-wing autocrats who ruled various Latin American and European

Castro's Love of Books

García Márquez has frequently been asked about the nature of his friendship with Cuban leader Fidel Castro. The writer always answers that the two men spend most of their time talking about literature. In this excerpt from an article written in 2006, García Márquez tells about Castro's love of reading books.

Books are another source of vital information [for Castro, in addition to newspapers and official documents]. He's an avid reader. No one understands where he finds enough time or what method he applies to read so much and so quickly, although he insists he uses none in particular. He frequently takes a book with him in the early hours and makes comments about it the following morning. He can read in English, but he doesn't speak it. He'd rather read in Spanish, and at any given time is willing to read whatever piece of paper with letters on it that falls into his hands. A regular reader of economic and historical topics, he also appreciates good literature and follows it very closely.

Gabriel García Márquez, "The Fidel Castro I Know." http://info.interactivist.net/article.pl?sid=06/08/03/155 4249&mode=nested&tid=16.

countries in the twentieth century. Among the most repressive and despicable, in his eyes, were Chile's Augusto Pinochet (who ruled from 1973 to 1981), Spain's Francisco Franco (1939–1975), and the Soviet Union's Joseph Stalin (1922–1953). García Márquez denounced these men in a number of newspaper articles over the years. But his broadest attack on the concept of repressive dictatorship was fictional, namely his novel *The Autumn of the Patriarch*.

Published in 1975, the book was the first large-scale project García Márquez tackled after the success of *One Hundred Years of Solitude* in the late 1960s. (In 1972 he had published a collection of short stories, and the following year he released *I Was Happy and Uninformed*, a collection of his newspaper articles from the previous twenty years.) *The Autumn of the Patriarch* tells the story of an unnamed despotic ruler whose image is an amalgamation, or combination, of several different real-life dictators. "My intention," García Márquez later explained, was always to make a synthesis of all the Latin American dictators, but especially those from the Caribbean. Nevertheless, the personality of Juan Vicente Gómez [a military general who ruled Venezuela between 1908 and 1935] was strong, in addition to the fact that he exercised a special fascination over me, that undoubtedly the Patriarch has much more of him than anyone else. In any case, the mental image that I have of both is the same. Which doesn't mean, of course, that he is the same character as the one in the book, but rather an idealization of his image.[51]

As the book's plot unfolds, the author shows how a repressive dictator inevitably corrupts everything he touches. At the same time, the paranoid title character feels that he cannot totally trust

García Márquez believed right-wing dictators such as the former leader of Chile, Augusto Pinochet, were dangerous and repressive.

anyone around him, so he becomes increasingly isolated and miserable. To emphasize this chilling isolation, García Márquez takes the reader inside the dictator's head, revealing his unwholesome thought processes in long, complicated, and sometimes disjointed sentences. Some readers found this approach overly complex, distracting, and disconcerting, while others viewed it as bold and innovative. Critic Allen Ruch, who falls into the second group, describes the book's style this way:

> A creature beautifully pure in his cruelty and despair, García Márquez's tyrant is locked in this poetic novel like a monstrous butterfly in a collection of atrocities. And the device that García Márquez uses to pin him down for examination is a relentless and overwhelming prose, a winding sheet of endless words twisting through the tyrant's head. . . . Composed of lengthy, unpunctuated sentences, the narrative is brutally swift in pace, its sharp points falling upon its subjects in a rain of daggers. It is this dense but fluid prose that makes *Autumn of the Patriarch* García Márquez's most challenging novel; but it also makes it one of his most exciting. . . . The narrative flow is breathtaking yet deliberately confusing, placing the reader in a nightmare labyrinth of time and space, and forcing one to construct the story from a collection of nonlinear fragments, [which writhe] through the minds of the characters and furiously lash the page, unleashing its torrent of horror and beauty.[52]

The Padilla Affair

Not long after the publication of *The Autumn of the Patriarch*, García Márquez began to divide his time between extended stays in Mexico City and in Bogotá. Continuing his political activism, he used some of his own money to establish a newsmagazine, *Alternativa*. Not surprisingly, it expressed a decidedly left-wing point of view on political and social issues. In 1977, García Márquez made another political statement by publishing *Operation Carlota*, a collection of essays discussing Cuban intervention in the African nation of Angola. The book largely supported Cuba's efforts to help local Communists come to power in Angola.

Particularly controversial was García Márquez's participation in a series of events that pitted Fidel Castro against the well-known Cuban poet Heberto Padilla (1932–2000). Back in 1971, Castro had imprisoned Padilla for speaking out against the government. Many people in Latin America, especially intellectuals, writers, and artists, protested, arguing that the arrest was a clear attack on free speech.

Dazzling Exaggerations

"I want to be a writer in my next reincarnation, [more to the point,] one like him [García Márquez], with those stubborn and persistent details that, like a philosopher's stone, give total credibility to his dazzling exaggerations."

—Fidel Castro, quoted in "A Review of García Márquez's Memoir."
www.counterpunch.org/castro10182003.html.

In contrast, García Márquez was far less vocal in his support for Padilla. He agreed that intellectuals should be allowed to speak their minds. But he also worried that too much criticism of the Cuban government might hurt the image of the Cuban Revolution, which he viewed as a major power for good in the region. "What we ought to do," he said shortly after Padilla was jailed,

> is to look at the revolution as an integral phenomenon, and see how the positive aspects infinitely outweigh the negative ones. Of course, manifestations such as the Padilla case are extremely dangerous, but they are obstacles that it shouldn't be hard to surmount. If not, it would indeed be grievous, because everything [good] that [the revolution has accomplished]—making people literate, giving them education and economic independence—is irreversible and will last much longer than Padilla and Fidel.[53]

Yet despite his pro-Castro stance, García Márquez ended up using his considerable influence to aid the imprisoned poet. In 1980, at García Márquez's urgings, Castro allowed Padilla to leave Cuba. A number of people praised the Colombian writer for helping to give the Padilla affair a happy ending. But others criticized García Márquez for not working harder to free other political prisoners held in Cuban jails.

A Narrow Escape

Ironically, less than a year after Padilla's release, García Márquez was suddenly in danger of becoming a political prisoner himself. Colombia's right-wing regime was experiencing mounting troubles with Communist insurgents who wanted to take over the government. Perhaps because of García Márquez's close ties with Castro and other Cuban Communists, military leaders in Colombia suddenly accused the writer of supporting the local rebels.

This charge was patently false. But an arrest warrant was issued for García Márquez, and he and Mercedes had to seek asylum in the Mexican embassy in Bogotá. From there, they flew to Mexico

García Márquez's support for Cuba and Castro led to his exile from Colombia and his relocation to Mexico City.

Death of a Matriarch

García Márquez likes to point out that longevity is in his genes, so to speak. In the first installment of his autobiography, published in 2003, he relates how the matriarch of his family, his mother Luisa, died in her late nineties, leaving behind many generations of offspring.

Her [excellent state of] health [as an adult] allowed her to celebrate her ninety-seventh birthday with eleven of her children and . . . sixty-five grand- children, eighty-eight great- grandchildren, and fourteen- great-great-grandchildren. Not counting those no one ever knew about. She died of natural causes on June 9, 2002, at eight- thirty in the evening, when we were already preparing to cele- brate her first century of life, and on the same day and almost at the same hour that I put the final period to these memoirs.

Gabriel García Márquez, *Living to Tell the Tale*, trans. Edith Grossman. New York: Knopf, 2003, p. 44.

City, which once more became their full-time home. The couple's narrow escape and flight to safety made headlines across the globe. Later in 1981, France, home of many longtime admirers of García Márquez, awarded him a highly prestigious award, the Legion of Honor, for his courage in the face of tyranny.

García Márquez appreciated the award and other similar acco- lades and gestures of support that he received in this period. But these honors could not erase the unpleasant reality he now faced. Although he had achieved fame, fortune, and widespread respect as a writer, he was an outcast from his native land. Fortunately for him, this unenviable situation was not destined to endure for very long. Practically no one, including García Márquez himself, was prepared for the sudden reversal of fortune that was about to occur. A small group of people whom he had never met, liv- ing in a faraway place he had never visited, were about to make a decision that would alter the course of his life. So momentous would that decision be that even his enemies would be forced to embrace him. Quite literally overnight, an annoying political exile would be transformed into a heroic native son.

Chapter 6

Literary Giant

Ⓞne morning early in 1982, Gabriel García Márquez was put-
tering around his house in Mexico City when the phone
rang. To his complete surprise, the caller was a representative of
the Swedish Academy, the prestigious cultural institution that is
best known for choosing the winners of the coveted Nobel Prizes
each year. (The prizes are awarded for achievements in literature,
physics, chemistry, economics, medicine, and world peace.) García
Márquez had been selected, the man said, to receive that year's
Nobel Prize for Literature. In its official statement about the prize,
the academy said it had chosen García Márquez in recognition of
"his novels and short stories, in which the fantastic and the realistic are combined in a richly composed world of imagination,
reflecting a continent's life and conflicts."[54]

A Long Overdue Reconciliation

Thrilled by the news, García Márquez found himself fielding calls
of congratulation from friends, fellow writers, and heads of state
around the world. Many of them commented that this great honor
reflected positively not only on the recipient, but also on Latin

In 1982, García Márquez was awarded the Nobel Prize for Literature. His mix of realism and the supernatural intrigued the judges.

American writers in general. In a sense, it signaled that the literature of the region had come of age and could stand beside that of Europe and the United States.

Even more important to García Márquez was the way his winning the prize swiftly ended his troubles with the Colombian government. There had recently been an election in the country. The new president, Belisario Bentancur, had promised to institute democratic reforms and conduct peace talks with local rebels. Bentancur immediately recognized that Colombia's political and cultural image would be significantly enhanced by association with García Márquez in his moment of glory. So the president reached out to the exiled author, inviting him to return to his native land and promising to protect him.

In the midst of this long overdue reconciliation, García Márquez, now about fifty-five, made the trip to Stockholm, Sweden, to accept his prize. In its official statement, the Nobel committee praised him for the high quality of his fiction and the importance of the political dimension in his writing, which, the committee said, derived from a lifelong commitment to caring about the plight of peoples living under political repression:

> For a long time, Latin American literature has shown a vigour as in few other literary spheres, having won acclaim in the cultural life of today. Many impulses and traditions cross each other . . . [and] blend into a spiced and life-giving brew from which García Márquez and other Spanish-American writers derive material and inspiration. The violent conflicts of a political nature—social and economic—raise the temperature of the intellectual climate. Like most of the other important writers in the Latin American world, García Márquez is

Frustrated by Terminlogy

In a 1982 interview, García Márquez commented on one of his pet peeves—what he sees as the misuse of the term "America" by people in the United States.

It bothers me that the people of the United States have appropriated the word America as if they were the *only* Americans. America, in fact, begins at the South Pole and ends at the North Pole. When residents of the United States call themselves Americans, they are telling us they think of themselves as the only Americans. Actually, those people are residents of a country without a name. . . . They should find a name, because right now they have none. We have the United States of Mexico, the United States of Brazil. But the United States? The United States of what? . . . As a partisan for Latin America, I can't help but feel resentful when North Americans appropriate the word American for themselves.

Quoted in Gene H. Bell-Villada, ed., *Conversations with Gabriel García Márquez.* Jackson: University Press of Mississippi, 2006, p. 98.

strongly committed, politically, on the side of the poor and the weak against domestic oppression and foreign economic exploitation.[55]

García Márquez had already established himself as a literary giant before he won the Nobel Prize. However, the award had the effect of officially confirming, as well as celebrating, that fact on a worldwide stage. He was now in a sense an elder statesman of the world literary scene. And in the years that followed, he lived up to that image by maintaining professional and social ties with writers, journalists, and educators in many countries. In addition to houses in Barranquilla and Cartagena in Colombia, he and Mercedes retained their residence in Mexico and established new ones in France and Spain. Meanwhile, he continued his prodigious output of writing, managing to strike a comfortable and productive balance between fiction and nonfiction.

Two New Novels

The first novel that García Márquez wrote after winning the Nobel Prize was published in the winter of 1985–1986. Titled *Love in the Time of Cholera*, it was based loosely on his parents' courtship in the 1920s. The two main characters—Florentino and Fermina —meet in their youth and fall in love. But life intervenes, they drift apart, and she marries another man. Only after Fermina's husband dies many years later is she reunited with Florentino, who has maintained his strong feelings for her for five decades.

As the author guides the reader through the torturous path the lovers must take to reach their ultimate happiness, he explores several universal themes. Among these, as the title suggests, is love, here presented as something well worth pursuing but also as a kind of emotional disease that can bring pain and suffering along the way. García Márquez also uses the story of the lovers to look at aging and death and how people try to cope with these inevitable realities.

Love in the Time of Cholera received widespread praise, including a favorable review by noted *New York Times* literary critic Thomas Pynchon. "Love is strange," he wrote in a penetrating analysis of the author's examination of the concept of eternal love, and as we grow older it gets stranger, until at some point mortality has come well within the frame of our attention, and there we are, suddenly caught between terminal dates [with death] while still talking a game of [eternal love]. Suppose, then, it were possible, not only to swear love "forever," but actually to follow through on it—to live a long, full, and authentic life based on such a vow, to put one's allotted stake of precious time where one's heart is? This is the extraordinary premise of Gabriel García Márquez's new novel . . . one on which he delivers, and triumphantly.[56]

By the time the initial reviews for *Love in the Time of Cholera* appeared, García Márquez was already hard at work on another novel. This time he chose to go back in time and take a fresh and unorthodox look at a Latin American hero. *The General in His Labyrinth*, which appeared in 1990, is a fictionalized account of Simón Bolívar, the great freedom fighter who helped to establish the nations of

García Márquez's novel The General in His Labyrinth *is a fictionalized account of Simón Bolívar, a South American revolutionary leader.*

Venezuela, Colombia, and Peru in the early 1800s. García Márquez concentrates on Bolívar's later years, again scrutinizing the pitiless aging process. In essence, the book is an uncompromising exploration of how the once great leader might have dealt with the ravages of sickness, poverty, and the loss of the respect and love of the peoples he had liberated.

In the News

As had been true throughout his writing career, the nonfiction García Márquez produced after winning the Nobel Prize was of a journalistic and/or political nature. In 1996, for instance, he published *News of a Kidnapping*, which exposed the brutality and wastefulness of the Colombian drug trade. He also bought a struggling

Colombian newsmagazine, *Cambio*, in 1999. For a long time he had dreamed of owning and running his own magazine, one in which he would not only report important stories, but also act as chief editor. This gave him the final say on what did and did not make it into print. And he was free to be as outspoken as he desired on any topic he chose.

Typical was one of the first articles the magazine published, in which García Márquez commented on the ongoing investigation by U.S. special prosecutor Kenneth Starr of President Bill Clinton's sexual tryst with White House intern Monica Lewinsky. García Márquez greatly admired Clinton and viewed the scandal surrounding the incident as both silly and a waste of taxpayers' money. In the *Cambio* article, the magazine's owner-editor-reporter called Starr a "fundamentalist" and charged that he secretly got sexually aroused by his investigation of Clinton's erotic escapade. "Is it fair," García Márquez asked, "that this rare example of the human species [Clinton] must squander his historic destiny just because he couldn't find a safe place to make love?"[57]

In 1999, García Márquez bought a struggling Colombian newsmagazine, Cambio, *so he could have an open forum to publish his most controversial thoughts on various topics.*

García Márquez Meets Bill Clinton

García Márquez's novels have universal appeal and have been read by many global heads of state, from Cuba's Fidel Castro to France's François Mitterrand to U.S. president Bill Clinton. García Márquez recalled discussing his novels with Clinton at a dinner party in 1995:

> The first thing you notice about William Jefferson Clinton is how tall he is. The second is the seductive power he has of making you feel . . . that he is someone you know well. The third is his sharp intelligence, which allows you to speak to him about anything at all. . . . I met him first at a dinner given by [American novelist and essayist] William Styron in his summer house on Martha's Vineyard in August 1995. During his first campaign, Clinton had mentioned that his favorite book was [my novel] *One Hundred Years of Solitude*. I said [during the campaign] that I thought he had said it simply to pull in the Latin vote. He had not forgotten. After greeting me on Martha's Vineyard, he at once assured me that what he said had been quite sincere.

The novelist noted that Clinton proceeded to recite the opening lines of the book word for word.

Gabriel García Márquez, "The Mysteries of Bill Clinton." www.salon.com/news/1999/02/cov_02news.html.

Former U.S. president Bill Clinton (right) is a fan of García Márquez's writings.

The Translator's Challenge

"You can be sure that the attempt to enter the mind of García Márquez is as exciting and challenging as the work of a translator gets."

—Edith Grossman, "On Translation and García Márquez." www.themodernword.com/gabo/gabo_PEN_grossman.html.

While he was writing about politics and news, at times García Márquez himself became the subject of news articles, including some he would have been happy to do without. In the same year he bought *Cambio*, for example, newspapers around the world announced that he had been diagnosed with lymphatic cancer (cancer of the lymph nodes, part of the body's immune system). García Márquez's doctors informed him that he faced a difficult struggle, but with vigorous treatments he could expect to live for at least several more years. The writer immediately began a treatment regimen based in clinics in Mexico City and Los Angeles. His visits to Los Angeles afforded him the chance to spend time with his son Rodrigo, who works as a filmmaker there.

Longing for "a Scrap of Life"

During the early stages of his cancer treatments, another, even more disturbing report about García Márquez's health made the news. In May 2000, a Peruvian newspaper, *La Republica*, printed a poem titled "La Marioneta" ("The Puppet"), attributed to him. The paper claimed that he was about to die and that the poem was his last farewell to his friends and family. "If for a moment God would forget that I am a rag doll and give me a scrap of life," the poem began,

> possibly I would not say everything that I think, but I would definitely think everything that I say. I would value things not for how much they are worth, but rather for what they mean. I would sleep little, dream more. I know that for each minute that we close our eyes we lose sixty seconds of light. . . . I would listen when the others speak, and how I would enjoy a good chocolate ice cream. If God would bestow on me a scrap

of life, I would dress simply, I would throw myself under the sun, exposing not only my body but also my soul. . . . I wouldn't let a single day go by without saying to people I love, that I love them.[58]

Many people, including several of García Márquez's old friends, were moved by these words and hastened to send him farewell wishes. Much to their surprise, however, they learned that the heartfelt poem was not written by García Márquez. Moreover, his health had not worsened, and he was not dying. It turned out that an obscure Mexican ventriloquist named Johnny Welch had written the poem for the puppet he used in his act, and an unidentified person had added García Márquez's name to the piece and spread the false rumor about the novelist's impending death.

García Márquez on the Past

García Márquez had no official comment about the bizarre incident, although in private he made sure to call friends and assure them that he was all right. His public remarks concentrated instead on his upcoming autobiography. The recent onset of cancer had made him increasingly aware of his own mortality, and he pondered how best to spend whatever time he had left. It seemed prudent to him to set down on paper the many memories of his rich, eventful life while he still had the energy to work.

The result was the publication of *Living to Tell the Tale*, the first of three projected volumes of memoirs, in 2003. The book begins with the incident in which his mother asked him to return with her to Aracataca to sell the family house. After seeing the village for the first time in several years, the young man is flooded by memories of his childhood, marking the start of the main narrative. The book then details his life up to 1955, when he was about twenty-seven.

Writing his memoirs forced García Márquez to reflect in great detail on how his life had changed over the years. In particular, he was struck by the tremendous contrast between his long periods of poverty and uncertainty and his ultimate achievement of success, fame, and independence. In an earlier interview, he had summarized what he saw as an amazing transformation:

For a long time, of course, things did not work out for me—almost the first 40 years of my life. I had financial problems; I had work problems. I had not made it as a writer or as anything else. It was a difficult time emotionally and psychologically. I had the idea that I was like an extra, that I did not count anywhere. And then, with *One Hundred Years of Solitude*, things turned. Now all this is going on without my being dependent on anyone.[59]

But even with success and independence, García Márquez came to realize, his life was fraught with setbacks and compromises.

A bookstore offers works by García Márquez. In 1999, newspapers reported García Márquez's battle with cancer.

These included the aging process, his declining health, and the need to follow his doctors' orders about dieting and exercise, both of which the writer found unpleasant. "I have to sit on [an exercise] bicycle in the morning," he complained. Also, "I am on an eternal diet. Half my life I couldn't eat what I wanted because I couldn't afford to, the other half because I have [to stick to] a diet."[60]

García Márquez on the Future

The author of *One Hundred Years of Solitude* is more upbeat when he considers the future, particularly the future of Latin American culture. During his long life, he says, he has watched many positive political and social developments in Latin America. After long periods of extreme poverty, hardship, and struggle, Colombia, Venezuela, Chile, and other countries in the region have worked their way into the modern, industrialized world. And Latin American thinkers, writers, and artists have achieved the same level of respect as their counterparts in Europe and the United States.

Part of this improvement in Latin America's status and image, García Márquez points out, was the result of enhanced lines of communication and understanding between both writers and ordinary people in Latin America and Europe. For many years, he says, people in other parts of the world looked down on Latin American culture, including its literature. This arrogant attitude made him "furious" because it was "an unfair analysis" of Latin America. "Our countries [in Latin America] are only 170 years old," he notes:

> European countries are much older than that and have gone through far more atrocious episodes than what we in Latin America are going through. That we should seem savage to them now! We have never had as barbarian a revolution as the French Revolution! The Swiss—cheese-makers who consider themselves great pacifists—were Europe's bloodiest mercenaries [hired soldiers] in the Middle Ages! Europeans had to go through long periods of bloodshed and violence to become what they are today. When we are as old as the

García Márquez's son Rodrigo holds the top-ranking Golden Leopard Award that he receved for his film Nine Lives *in 2005. García Márquez visited Rodrigo in Los Angeles while receiving treatment for cancer there.*

European countries, we'll be much more advanced than Europe is now, because we will have both our experience and theirs to draw on.[61]

Regarding the future of Latin American artistic expression, García Márquez expresses the hope that writers from the region will continue to turn out well-written and thought-provoking works. He also talks frequently about the medium of film, an art form for which he penned several screenplays. A few of these were made into films, though before 2005 none of his novels had made it to the big screen. In that year he sold the script for a movie version of his novel *Love in the Time of Cholera*, which British director Mike Newell began working on with an international cast. Production wrapped in December 2006 for a 2007 release.

Moral and Spiritual Authority

"Right now we need someone with great moral and spiritual authority. Gabo [García Márquez] is the one person who could go out and stand between the two sides shooting at one another and say 'No more,' and everyone would listen."

—Jamie Márquez, García Márquez's brother, quoted in "The Power of Gabriel Garcia Marquez." www.themodernword.com/gabo/gabo_power.html.

So far García Márquez has not commented on the fact that the first movie version of any of his novels was made in English rather than Spanish and by a European rather than Latin American director. However, García Márquez has expressed the opinion that Latin American filmmakers possess an almost unlimited potential to make great films. They have not yet fulfilled that potential, he says, in part because most films made in the region have not earned a lot of money at the box office. This has kept the amount of money invested in Latin American film production relatively low. "I'd like to see filmmaking as an artistic expression in Latin America valued the same way as our literature is now," he says:

> We have very fine literature, but it has taken a long time to be recognized. It has been a very hard struggle. . . . The same is beginning to happen with film. There are now good films being made in Latin America. And this is being done not through great productions with a lot of capital [money]. It is done within our own means and with our own methods. And the films are appearing at the international [film] festivals [such as Cannes, in France] and are being nominated for prizes. But they still have to conquer their own audience here. The problem lies with the big distributors. They need to spend

A riverboat specially built for the movie Love in the Time of Cholera *is used during filming in the Caribbean in 2006.*

a lot of money to promote unknown films. . . . The day our films make money, the whole focus will change. We saw it in literature. We will see it in films in the years ahead.[62]

As for his own future, García Márquez, aged eighty and candid as always, admits that it is uncertain. "The year 2005 was the first in my life when I did not write a single line," he says. This was partly because of his declining health, but also because he just did not have any urgent flashes of inspiration. "If tomorrow a new novel occurred to me," he asserts, "that would be fantastic! With the [writing] practice I have, I could write another novel without further problems." But it would have to be based on a subject with a lot of substance, he adds. "People notice when one has not put the guts in it."[63]

Notes

Introduction: A Literary Earthquake

1. Quoted in Raymond L. Williams, *Gabriel García Márquez*. Boston: Twayne, 1984, p. 1.
2. Ruben Pelayo, *Gabriel García Márquez: A Critical Companion*. Westport, CT: Greenwood, 2001, pp. 32–33.
3. Quoted in Gene H. Bell-Villada, ed., *Conversations with Gabriel García Márquez*. Jackson: University Press of Mississippi, 2006, p. 108.
4. Williams, *Gabriel García Márquez*, pp. 156–57.
5. Quoted in Frank Bajak, "García Márquez Delights Bill Clinton, Others at Tribute." www.suburbanchicagonews.com/newssun/entertainment/314940,5_WA27_garciamarquez.article.

Chapter 1: Ghosts of Childhood

6. Gabriel García Márquez, *Living to Tell the Tale*, trans. Edith Grossman. New York: Knopf, 2003, p. 45.
7. Pelayo, *Gabriel García Márquez*, p. 22.
8. Allen B. Ruch, "The Uncertain Old Man Whose Real Existence Was the Simplest of His Enigmas." www.themodernword.com/gabo/gabo_biography.html.
9. García Márquez, *Living to Tell the Tale*, pp. 14–15.
10. Quoted in Bell-Villada, *Conversations*, pp. 117–18.
11. Quoted in Ruch, "Uncertain Old Man."
12. Quoted in Williams, *Gabriel García Márquez*, p. 6.
13. García Márquez, *Living to Tell the Tale*, pp. 75–76.
14. Quoted in Bell-Villada, *Conversations*, p. 114.
15. Quoted in Bell-Villada, *Conversations*, p. 117.
16. García Márquez, *Living to Tell the Tale*, pp. 90–91.
17. García Márquez, *Living to Tell the Tale*, p. 125.

Chapter 2: Finding His Way

18. García Márquez, *Living to Tell the Tale*, p. 95.

19. García Márquez, *Living to Tell the Tale*, p. 189.
20. Quoted in Jon Lee Anderson, "The Power of Gabriel García Márquez." www.themodernword.com/gabo/gabo_power. html.
21. Franz Kafka, *The Metamorphosis*, trans. Stanley Corngold. New York: Bantam, 1972, p. 3.
22. Quoted in Ruch, "Uncertain Old Man."
23. Williams, *Gabriel García Márquez*, p. 8.
24. Quoted in Ruch, "Uncertain Old Man."
25. Quoted in Bell-Villada, *Conversations*, p. 83.
26. García Márquez, *Living to Tell the Tale*, p. 4.
27. García Márquez, *Living to Tell the Tale*, pp. 3–4.
28. García Márquez, *Living to Tell the Tale*, p. 5.

Chapter 3: World Traveler

29. Quoted in Williams, *Gabriel García Márquez*, p. 8.
30. Pelayo, *Gabriel García Márquez*, p. 35.
31. Luis Harss, "Gabriel García Márquez, or the Lost Chord," in Luis Harss and Barbara Dohmann, *Into the Mainstream: Conversations with Latin-American Writers*. New York: Harper and Row, 1967, p. 323.
32. Quoted in Bell-Villada, *Conversations*, p. 82.
33. Quoted in Harold Bloom, ed., *Gabriel García Márquez: Modern Critical Views*. New York: Chelsea House, 1989, p. 12.
34. Gabriel García Márquez, "Gabriel García Márquez Meets Ernest Hemingway." www.nytimes.com/books/99/07/04/specials/ hemingway-marquez.html.
35. García Márquez, "Gabriel García Márquez Meets Ernest Hemingway."
36. Williams, *Gabriel García Márquez*, p. 11.

Chapter 4: Breakthrough and Fame

37. Quoted in Ruch, "Uncertain Old Man."
38. Quoted in Ruch, "Uncertain Old Man."
39. Harss, "Gabriel García Márquez," p. 312.
40. Harss, "Gabriel García Márquez," p. 313.
41. Gabriel García Márquez, *One Hundred Years of Solitude*, trans. Gregory Rabassa. New York: HarperCollins, 1970, p. 1.

42. Williams, *Gabriel García Márquez*, p. 74.
43. Quoted in Williams, *Gabriel García Márquez*, p. 79.
44. Quoted in Bell-Villada, *Conversations*, p. 111.
45. BBC, "One Hundred Years of Solitude, by Gabriel García Márquez." www.bbc.co.uk/dna/h2g2/alabaster/A662997.

Chapter 5: Political Activist

46. Ruch, "Uncertain Old Man."
47. Quoted in Bell-Villada, *Conversations*, p. 97.
48. Gabriel García Márquez, "The Fidel Castro I Know." http://info.interactivist.net/article.pl?sid=06/08/03/1554249&mode=nested&tid=16.
49. Quoted in Bell-Villada, *Conversations*, p. 101.
50. Fidel Castro, "A Review of García Márquez's Memoir." www.counterpunch.org/castro10182003.html.
51. Quoted in Allen B. Ruch, "Gabo: Works of Fiction." www.themodernword.com/gabo/gabo_works_fiction.html.
52. Ruch, "Gabo."
53. Quoted in Bell-Villada, *Conversations*, p. 54.

Chapter 6: Literary Giant

54. Quoted in "Nobel Prize in Literature, 1982." http://nobel-prize.org/nobel_prizes/literature/laureates/1982.
55. "Press Release for Nobel Prize in Literature, 1982." http://nobel-prize.org/nobel_prizes/literature/laureates/1982/press.html.
56. Thomas Pynchon, "The Heart's Eternal Vow: A Review of Gabriel García Márquez's *Love in the Time of Cholera*." www.themodernword.com/pynchon/pynchon_essays_cholera.html.
57. Quoted in Associated Press, *"Cambio."* www.themodernword.com/gabo/cambio.html.
58. Quoted in Alex Boese, "Gabriel García Márquez's Final Farewell." www.museumofhoaxes.com/marquez.html.
59. Quoted in Joan Mellen, *Literary Masters: Gabriel García Márquez*. Detroit: Gale, 2000, pp. 125–26.
60. Quoted in Mellen, *Literary Masters*, p. 126.
61. Quoted in Bell-Villada, *Conversations*, pp. 108–109.

62. Quoted in Mellen, *Literary Masters*, pp. 130–31.

63. Quoted in "Colombian Nobel Laureate García Márquez Says He Has Stopped Writing." http://newsfromrussia. com/culture/2006/01/29/72012.html.

Important Dates

1927 (or 1928?)
Gabriel García Márquez is born in the small Colombian town of Aracataca.

1935
At about age eight, García Márquez moves to Barranquilla, west of Aracataca, and begins attending school.

1948
García Márquez takes part in street riots that mark the beginning of "the Violence," a turbulent period of civil strife in Colombia.

1952
García Márquez publishes his first novel, *Leaf Storm*.

1954
García Márquez lands a job with the Colombian newspaper *El Espectador*.

1958
García Márquez marries Mercedes Barcha Pardo, a resident of Barranquilla.

1959
Working as a journalist, García Márquez goes to Cuba to cover the successful Cuban Revolution led by Fidel Castro.

1967
García Márquez finishes writing his masterpiece, *One Hundred Years of Solitude*, which makes him a world-renowned author.

1975
García Márquez publishes his next novel, *The Autumn of the Patriarch*.

1980
At the urging of his friend García Márquez, Castro frees Cuban poet Heberto Padilla, who had been jailed for dissenting against the government.

1982

García Márquez wins the Nobel Prize for Literature.

1986

García Márquez publishes *Love in the Time of Cholera*, a novel loosely based on his parents' courtship.

1996

In a nonfiction work titled *News of a Kidnapping*, García Márquez reveals the brutality of the Colombian drug trade.

2003

García Márquez publishes *Living to Tell the Tale*, the first installment of his long-awaited autobiography.

2007

The film version of *Love in the Time of Cholera*, for which García Márquez himself wrote the screenplay, is released.

For More Information

Books

Gene H. Bell-Villada, ed., *Conversations with Gabriel García Márquez*. Jackson: University Press of Mississippi, 2006. A valuable collection of interviews of Gabriel García Márquez by various scholars and critics.

Susan M. Darraj, *Gabriel García Márquez*. New York: Chelsea House, 2006. A good, short biography of García Márquez.

Rejina Janes, *"One Hundred Years of Solitude": Modes of Reading*. Boston: G.K. Hall, 1991. Explores the literary importance, themes, plot, and characters of García Márquez's masterpiece.

Efrain Kristal, ed., *The Cambridge Companion to the Latin American Novel*. New York: Cambridge University Press, 2005. Examines the works and literary history of the most important Latin American writers, including García Márquez.

Gabriel García Márquez, *Living to Tell the Tale*. Trans. Edith Grossman. New York: Knopf, 2003. The first installment of García Márquez's autobiography.

Joan Mellen, *Literary Masters: Gabriel García Márquez*. Detroit: Gale, 2000. A collection of articles and essays examining García Márquez, his life, his works, his politics, his influences, and more.

Ruben Pelayo, *Gabriel García Márquez: A Critical Companion*. Westport, CT: Greenwood, 2001. Devotes a chapter of explanatory and critical commentary to each of García Márquez's major novels.

Internet Sources

Gabriel García Márquez, "The Fidel Castro I Know." http://info. interactivist.net/article.pl?sid=06/08/03/1554249&mode= nested&tid=16. García Márquez presents an enlightening description of the controversial relationship between him and the Cuban dictator.

Gabriel García Márquez, "Nobel Prize Lecture." http://nobelprize.org/nobel_prizes/literature/laureates/1982/marquez-lecture-e.html. A transcript of García Márquez's speech on accepting the 1982 Nobel Prize in Literature.

New York Times Online, "Gabriel García Márquez Meets Ernest Hemingway." http://query.nytimes.com/gst/fullpage.html?res=940CEFD9163BF935A15754C0A967948260. A delightful essay written by García Márquez in which he recalls the only time he saw his idol Ernest Hemingway in person.

Allen B. Ruch, "The Uncertain Old Man Whose Real Existence Was the Simplest of His Enigmas." www.themodernword.com/gabo/gabo_biography.html. An excellent, detailed biography of García Márquez, including a great deal about the influence of Colombian politics on his life and work.

Index

Picture Credits

About the Author

Historian and award-winning writer Don Nardo has published many volumes of both single and multiple biography, among his subjects Ramesses II, Pericles, Aristotle, Philip II, Confucius, Julius Caesar, Cicero, Cleopatra, Tycho Brahe, Ivan the Terrible, Thomas Jefferson, Charles Darwin, Andrew Johnson, H.G. Wells, Queen Victoria, Franklin D. Roosevelt, and Adolf Hitler. Mr. Nardo also writes screenplays and teleplays and composes music. He resides in Massachusetts with his wife, Christine.